Functional Skills

English

Level 2

This CGP book covers everything you'll need for success in Level 2 Functional Skills English, whichever exam board you're studying.

Every topic is explained with clear, concise notes — and there's a huge range of practice questions and test-style tasks (with detailed answers) to help you make sure you're fully prepared for the final tests.

Since 1995, CGP has helped millions of students do well in their tests and exams. Our books cover dozens of subjects for all ages — at the best prices you'll find anywhere!

Study & Test Practice

Contents

Introduction

What is Functional English? 1

How To Use This Book 2

Using a Dictionary 3

Part 1 — Reading

Section 1 — How Ideas are Presented

The Purpose of Texts 4

Reading Between the Lines 10

Spotting Different Types of Text..14

Spotting Presentational Features 16

Spotting Language Techniques 20

Identifying Tone and Style 24

Section 2 — Finding Information From Texts

Selecting Texts..26

Picking Out the Main Points..28

Reading for Detail..30

Using Information 32

Using More Than One Text 34

Reading Test Practice

Different Types of Question 36

Reading Test Advice 39

Practice Reading Tests 40

Answers to the Reading Questions 64

Part 2 — Writing

Section 1 — Writing Structure and Planning

Knowing Your Audience and Purpose..68

Planning Your Answer..70

Writing and Checking Your Answer..72

Using Paragraphs..74

Section 2 — Choosing the Right Language and Format

Writing Emails 76

Writing Letters 78

Writing Articles 80

Writing Reports 82

Writing Leaflets 84

Writing Persuasively 86

Writing About Your Opinions 88

Section 3 — Using Grammar

Using Sentences 90

Using Joining Words to Add Detail 92

Using Joining Words to Link Ideas 94

Using Different Verb Tenses 96

Common Mistakes With Verbs 100

Section 4 — Using Correct Punctuation

Punctuating Sentences 102

Using Commas 104

Using Apostrophes 106

Using Inverted Commas 108

Section 5 — Using Correct Spelling

Spelling Tricks 110

Making Plurals 112

Adding Prefixes and Suffixes 114

Common Spelling Mistakes 116

Commonly Confused Words 118

Writing Test Practice

Writing Test Advice 122

Practice Writing Tests 123

Answers to the Writing Questions 133

Glossary 141

Index 143

Published by CGP

Editors:
Alex Fairer
Rachel Grocott
Holly Poynton
Matt Topping

With thanks to Glenn Rogers for the proofreading.
With thanks to Heather Hill for the copyright research.

Acknowledgements:

With thanks to iStockphoto.com for permission to reproduce the images on pages 38, 46 and 50.

All names, places and incidents are fictitious, any resemblance to actual events or persons is entirely coincidental.

ISBN: 978 1 78294 630 4

Printed by Elanders Ltd, Newcastle upon Tyne.
Clipart from Corel®

Text, design, layout and original illustrations © Coordination Group Publications Ltd. (CGP) 2015
All rights reserved.

Photocopying more than one chapter of this book is not permitted. Extra copies are available from CGP.
0800 1712 712 • www.cgpbooks.co.uk

What is Functional English?

Functional Skills are a set of qualifications

1) They're designed to give you the **skills** you need in **everyday life**.

2) There are **three** Functional Skills **subjects** — **English**, **Maths** and **ICT**.

3) You may have to sit **tests** in **one**, **two** or all **three** of these subjects.

4) Functional Skills has **five levels** — **Entry Level 1-3**, **Level 1** and **Level 2**.

This book is for Functional English

1) There are **three** parts to English — **speaking and listening**, **reading** and **writing**.

2) To get a Functional Skills English qualification, you need to **pass all three parts**.

3) You can take your reading and writing tests on a **computer** (onscreen) or on **paper**.

4) This book covers the **reading** and **writing** parts of **Functional English Level 2**.

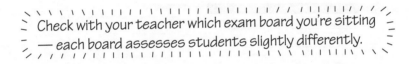

Check with your teacher which exam board you're sitting — each board assesses students slightly differently.

There are two tests and a controlled assessment

1) **Speaking and listening** is tested by a **controlled assessment** in class.

2) Reading and writing are tested in **two separate tests**.

3) You might take your test on a **computer** (onscreen) or on **paper**.

Reading

- In the **test**, you have to **read three or four texts** and **answer questions** on them.

- Some questions might be **multiple choice** (you choose the correct answer).

- Some questions might ask you to **write** your **answer**.

- You **don't** have to write in **full sentences**.

- You **won't** lose marks if you make **spelling**, **punctuation** or **grammar mistakes**.

Writing

- In the **test**, you will be asked to write **two texts**.

- These **two texts** will usually be **different**, for example a **letter** and an **article**.

- You **will lose marks** if your spelling, punctuation or grammar are **incorrect**.

How To Use This Book

This book summarises everything you need to know

1) This book is designed to help you **go over** what you're already learning in class.

2) Use it along with any **notes** and **resources** your teacher has given you.

3) You can work through this book from **start** to **finish**...

4) ...or you can just **target the topics** that you're **not sure** about.

Use this book to revise and test yourself

1) This book is split into **two parts** — **reading** and **writing**.

2) The topics in each part are usually **spread over two pages**:

Here's the title of the topic.

On the left-hand page there's all the important information for each topic.

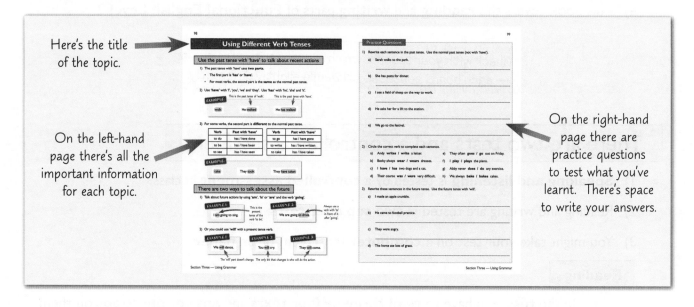

On the right-hand page there are practice questions to test what you've learnt. There's space to write your answers.

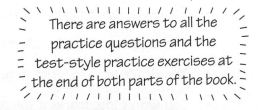

There are answers to all the practice questions and the test-style practice exercises at the end of both parts of the book.

There's lots of test-style practice

1) There are **test-style practice exercises** at the **end** of both parts of the book.

2) These exercises are based on **actual Functional Skills assessments**.

3) This means that the questions are **similar** to the ones you'll get in the **real tests**.

4) The **reading tests** have a **mix** of **question types** with **space** to write your answers.

5) The **writing tests** have space for a **plan**, but you'll need **extra paper** for your full answer.

Using a Dictionary

You can use a dictionary in the test

1) You can use a dictionary to look up the **meaning** of a tricky word.

2) Or you can look up a word to check its **spelling**.

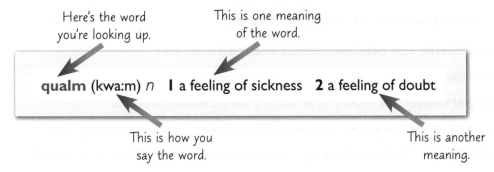

Here's the word you're looking up.

This is one meaning of the word.

qualm (kwa:m) *n* **1** a feeling of sickness **2** a feeling of doubt

This is how you say the word.

This is another meaning.

Practise using a dictionary before the test

1) The words in a **dictionary** are listed in **alphabetical order**.

2) That means all the words beginning with '**a**' are **grouped together**, then all the words beginning with '**b**' and so on.

3) Each **letter** in the word is also listed in **alphabetical order**.

4) When you're looking up a word, check the words in **bold** at the **top** of **each page**.

5) These words help you work out which **page** you need to **turn to**.

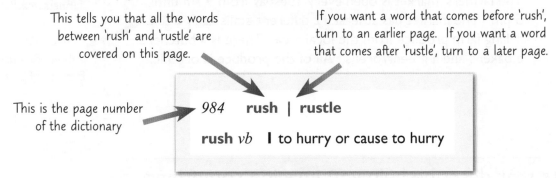

This tells you that all the words between 'rush' and 'rustle' are covered on this page.

If you want a word that comes before 'rush', turn to an earlier page. If you want a word that comes after 'rustle', turn to a later page.

This is the page number of the dictionary

984   **rush | rustle**

rush *vb* **1** to hurry or cause to hurry

Don't use a dictionary all the time

1) Dictionaries can be **helpful**, but **don't** use them **too often**.

2) Looking up **lots** of words will **slow you down** in the test...

3) ...so try to **learn** the **spelling** of **tricky** words **beforehand**.

4) Or you could think of a **word** that means the **same thing** that's **easier** to spell.

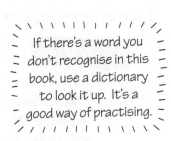

If there's a word you don't recognise in this book, use a dictionary to look it up. It's a good way of practising.

The Purpose of Texts

Texts have different purposes

1) A text is a **piece of writing**. Every text has a **purpose**.

2) A **purpose** is the **reason** why the text has been written.

3) These are the **main purposes** you could come across:

- **Texts that inform**. For example, a leaflet about a theme park.

- **Texts that describe**. For example, a review describing a hotel.

- **Texts that persuade**. For example, an advert for a cleaning product.

- **Texts that argue**. For example, a letter protesting about a school closing down.

- **Texts that discuss**. For example, a report about how much traffic is on the roads.

- **Texts that instruct**. For example, a recipe for making apple pie.

- **Texts that advise**. For example, a web page telling you how to save money.

Texts that inform tell you about something

Texts that inform are full of **facts**. **Facts** are statements that can be **proved**.

> The farmers' market is open every Tuesday from 9 am until 5 pm. The market has at least 12 different stalls each week selling farm produce from the local area. There is a butcher's, a baker's and a greengrocer's. All of the produce is organic.

This text is informing the reader about a farmers' market.

Informative writing often uses facts and figures.

Texts that describe help you imagine something

Descriptive writing uses lots of **adjectives** (describing words).

> The market is held on a wide street filled with market stalls. Each stall is overflowing with fresh vegetables, beautiful cakes or colourful jars of jam.

This text is describing a market.

Adjectives like 'wide', 'fresh', 'beautiful' and 'colourful' help you imagine what the market is like.

Read the text below, and then answer the questions underneath.

Stanhope Community Choir

We are a local choir based at Stanhope Community Centre. We rehearse between 7 and 9 pm on Tuesday evenings. The choir is made up of 80 people from the age of 16 to 85. There is also a junior choir for children aged between 6 and 16. The junior choir rehearses on Saturday mornings at 9 am.

Our history:

The choir is a charitable organisation that was set up in 2008 by Mark Patel. Mark was the conductor of Stanhope Choral Society. He wanted to create a choir that would attract people from all walks of life and would bring people from all over Stanhope together.

How it works:

People can come to the choir to learn to sing as part of a large group. We sing a mixture of popular and choral music. You don't need to be able to read music to join.

Performances:

We perform at the Stanhope Festival every year. We also perform carols in the town square at Christmas and sing at the county show in May.

For more information, visit our website: www.stanhopecommunitychoir.co.uk

1) Find the **main** purpose of this text, then select some text to support your answer.

Main purpose ....

....

Example from the text ....

....

2) Name two places where the choir performs.

Place 1:...

Place 2:...

3) In what year was the choir started?

....

The Purpose of Texts

Texts that persuade try to convince the reader to do something

1) Persuasive texts sometimes use **words** that make the reader **feel** something.

2) They might also use **facts** to sound more **convincing**.

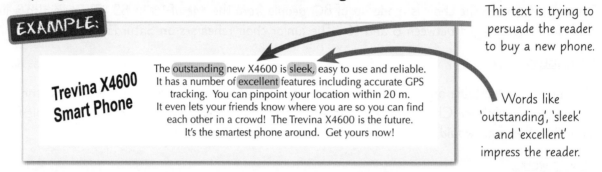

EXAMPLE:

Trevina X4600 Smart Phone

The outstanding new X4600 is sleek, easy to use and reliable. It has a number of excellent features including accurate GPS tracking. You can pinpoint your location within 20 m. It even lets your friends know where you are so you can find each other in a crowd! The Trevina X4600 is the future. It's the smartest phone around. Get yours now!

This text is trying to persuade the reader to buy a new phone.

Words like 'outstanding', 'sleek' and 'excellent' impress the reader.

Texts that argue want the reader to agree with an opinion

1) Texts that argue make **one opinion** very clear.

2) They often use **facts** to back up the argument and strong language to show how they feel.

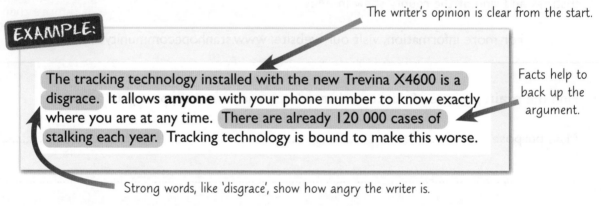

The writer's opinion is clear from the start.

EXAMPLE:

The tracking technology installed with the new Trevina X4600 is a disgrace. It allows **anyone** with your phone number to know exactly where you are at any time. There are already 120 000 cases of stalking each year. Tracking technology is bound to make this worse.

Facts help to back up the argument.

Strong words, like 'disgrace', show how angry the writer is.

Texts that discuss use evidence to reach a conclusion

1) Texts that discuss give **more than one opinion**.

2) They often look at **both sides** of an argument and reach a **conclusion**.

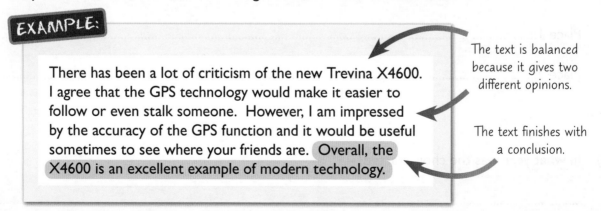

EXAMPLE:

There has been a lot of criticism of the new Trevina X4600. I agree that the GPS technology would make it easier to follow or even stalk someone. However, I am impressed by the accuracy of the GPS function and it would be useful sometimes to see where your friends are. Overall, the X4600 is an excellent example of modern technology.

The text is balanced because it gives two different opinions.

The text finishes with a conclusion.

Read the text below, and then answer the questions underneath.

Minna Williams is a disgrace by Jo Timms

I couldn't believe my ears yesterday when I heard Minna Williams speaking on the radio. The wife of the American politician Truman Williams said quite clearly that she thought women should stay at home and shouldn't work. She also said that women who do work 'don't deserve to be paid the same as men'. Is she really prepared to go back on one hundred years of fighting for equal rights?

Minna Williams is a housewife with five children. She has never worked. That is her choice and it is fine by me. But what she said yesterday was completely unacceptable. She implied that women are weaker than men in every way and do not deserve to be recognised as equals. Millions of women all over the world work to support themselves and their families. Women are just as capable as men, and should be paid exactly the same as men in the same jobs.

In some countries today, women are treated like second-class citizens. They are not even given the opportunity to learn or to work. Mrs Williams has grown up in a country where she is treated as an equal and where she could choose to work or not. She is one of the lucky ones, but she is encouraging young women to throw away those opportunities. She is a disgrace and doesn't deserve to call herself a woman.

1) Minna Williams thinks that:

   a)   Women are second-class citizens

   b)   Women shouldn't work

   c)   Women should be paid more than men

   d)   Women should be treated as equals

2) The writer thinks that:

   a)   Minna Williams is right

   b)   Minna Williams should get a job

   c)   Minna Williams is a second-class citizen

   d)   Minna Williams is wrong

3) What is the full name of Minna Williams's husband?

....

4) Find the **main** purpose of this text, then select some text to support your answer.

   Main purpose ....

   ....

   Example from the text ....

   ....

The Purpose of Texts

Texts that instruct tell you exactly what to do

1) Texts that instruct give the reader **instructions** to follow.

2) They are often split up into **numbered lists** or **bullet points**.

3) They use **clear language** so they are easy to understand.

EXAMPLE:

- Deal out seven cards to each player.
- Each player may discard one card that they do not want.

Simple language makes these instructions easy to follow.

Each instruction has a separate bullet point.

Texts that advise suggest how to do something

Texts that advise give you **tips** about something.

EXAMPLE:

HOW TO CHOOSE A NEW CAR

Here are some top tips for choosing a new car.

- Think about how much you want to spend. Making a budget makes it easier to decide what car to buy.
- Think about what you need it for. For example, if you have a big family, you'll need a large car.

These sentences are giving advice. They are suggesting how to do something.

Texts can have more than one purpose

1) Sometimes texts have **two or more** purposes.

2) For example, a text might **persuade** and **inform**, or **inform** and **describe**.

EXAMPLE:

UK Aid helps homeless people in the UK. Many of them have problems with alcohol and drugs, but they all deserve a chance. We run drop-in centres where homeless people can feel safe, get help and learn new skills. A donation of £3 a month helps us change lives. Change a life. Support UK Aid.

This text informs you about UK Aid.

It also persuades you to donate to UK Aid.

Read the texts below, and then answer the questions underneath each one.

Sporting success leads to increase in road cycling

The British cycling team were very successful at the Cycling World Championships this summer. The British team picked up 12 gold medals, 4 silver medals and a bronze medal at the championships in Hamburg, Germany. Ever since, there has been a noticeable rise in the number of people out and about on their bikes.

Cycling is popular for a number of reasons. It's cheap, it's a great way to get around and it keeps you fit. David Branford of the British cycling team said, "It's fabulous to see so many people enjoying cycling. Cycling is a fantastic sport. I'd like to see more kids getting involved, then Britain can continue to succeed internationally at cycling in the future."

So why not have a go yourself? Most people have a bike lying around in a shed or garage. Get it out, fix it up and get out and about. Cycling couldn't be easier. It's just like riding a bike!

1) Find **two** purposes of this text. Choose an example from the text to support your answer.

Purpose 1 ....

Example...

....

Purpose 2 ....

Example...

....

Weekend Guide to Paris - Sight Number 5

5. The Eiffel Tower

The Eiffel Tower is an architectural beauty. People come from all over Europe to see the best view in Paris. You can see the elegant Louvre art gallery, the River Seine snaking its way through the heart of the bustling city and the bridges filled with people and traffic. The view is unforgettable. Sadly, so are the queues. If you don't want to wait for 2 hours to get to the top you need to get there early. Young, fit people might consider climbing the stairs to avoid queuing for the lift. Tickets cost between €5 and €15.

2) Find **two** purposes of this text. Choose an example from the text to support your answer.

Purpose 1 ....

Example...

....

Purpose 2 ....

Example...

....

Reading Between the Lines

Facts are statements that can be proved

1) Some texts contain **facts** and **statistics**.

2) Statistics are **facts** that are based on **research** or **surveys**.

3) Statistics are usually written as **numbers** or **percentages**.

4) Phrases like '**experts say**', '**research shows**', '**surveys show**' often introduce facts.

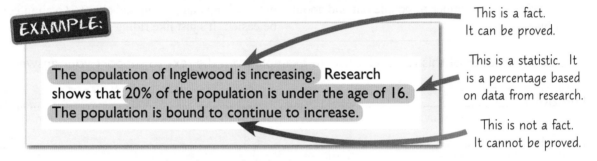

EXAMPLE:

The population of Inglewood is increasing. Research shows that 20% of the population is under the age of 16. The population is bound to continue to increase.

This is a fact. It can be proved.

This is a statistic. It is a percentage based on data from research.

This is not a fact. It cannot be proved.

An opinion is something the writer thinks

1) Opinions **aren't** true or untrue. They are just **beliefs** and **can't** be proved.

2) Phrases like '**I think**', '**I believe**' or '**many people say**' show a statement is an opinion.

3) Opinions can be **presented** to look like facts. This makes them seem more **believable**.

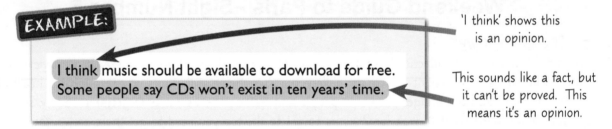

EXAMPLE:

I think music should be available to download for free. Some people say CDs won't exist in ten years' time.

'I think' shows this is an opinion.

This sounds like a fact, but it can't be proved. This means it's an opinion.

4) If you're **not sure** whether something is a fact or an opinion, think about whether it can be **proved** or not. If it **can**, it is a **fact**. If it **can't**, it is an **opinion**.

Some writers twist statistics to support their argument

Some writers might **twist** statistics to back up their **point of view**.

EXAMPLE:

100% of people like my band.

This seems unlikely. It might be true but we don't know how many people were asked. The writer might have only asked the people in the band.

Practice Questions

1) Read each statement and write **'fact'** or **'opinion'** next to each one to say whether the statement is **presented** as a fact or an opinion.

   a) 'Research shows that 60% of the UK population are overweight' ....

   b) 'Men are generally better at DIY than women' ....

   c) 'I think 9 out of 10 people would say they like chocolate' ....

   d) 'Surveys show children with siblings are better at sharing' ....

   Read the text below and then answer the questions underneath.

The success of the smoking ban

In July 2007 smoking was banned in public places in England. This was the most sensible decision made by the government in years. The ban was popular with the majority of the population. In a recent survey, 78% of people said they still support the smoking ban.

It is now much more pleasant to go into a pub or a restaurant. Before the ban, pubs were filled with smoke which made you cough and made your hair and clothes smell. However, according to a recent study, 16% of bar and pub owners have noticed a significant drop in business because smokers are staying at home rather than going out for a drink.

Making smoking in public places illegal has had a positive impact on people's health. Since the ban 400 000 people in England have given up smoking and the number of people suffering heart attacks has fallen by more than 2%. The benefits have also affected non-smokers. For example, the number of children suffering from asthma has decreased by around 20%.

2) There are six statements from the text in the table below. Put a **tick** next to each statement to show which are presented as **facts** and which are presented as **opinions**.

	Fact	Opinion
In July 2007 smoking was banned in public places in England		
This was the most sensible decision made by the government in years		
In a recent survey, 78% of people said they still support the smoking ban		
It is now much more pleasant to go into a pub or a restaurant		
Since the ban 400 000 people in England have given up smoking		
The number of children suffering from asthma has decreased by around 20%		

3) Give **another** example of a statistic from the article that is **not** in the table.

   ....

   ....

   ....

Reading Between the Lines

Writing isn't always balanced

1) Sometimes a writer has a **point of view** (an opinion) they want to get across.

2) They try to **influence** the reader by only giving their **opinion**. This is called **bias**.

3) A biased text might **exaggerate** something or **ignore** the other side of the argument.

EXAMPLE:

> North Coast Trains is the worst train company in Britain. Their trains are never on time, and they are always overcrowded. Last week I had to stand for a six-hour journey, which was just great.

The first sentence is an opinion. Many people might disagree with it.

The text ignores the fact that other train companies have trains that aren't on time and are overcrowded.

The writer doesn't actually mean it was great. They mean the opposite. This is irony. Here it makes the reader understand how angry the writer is feeling.

Biased texts use different methods to influence the reader

1) A text might use **humour** to **entertain** the reader. This makes the reader **like** the writer.

EXAMPLE:

> The new Hadawi sports car is the worst car I've ever driven. The engine is pathetic — I think my three-legged tortoise could probably move faster.

This is a funny image. If the reader likes the writer, they are more likely to agree with their opinion.

2) Biased texts might use **strong language** to make the reader **agree** with the writer.

EXAMPLE:

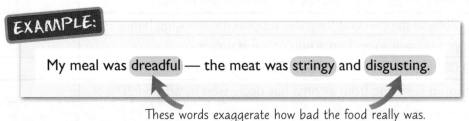

> My meal was dreadful — the meat was stringy and disgusting.

These words exaggerate how bad the food really was.

3) Biased texts might make claims that **aren't supported** with **evidence**.

EXAMPLE:

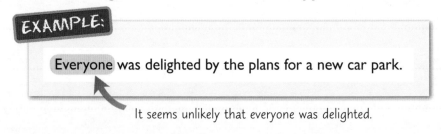

> Everyone was delighted by the plans for a new car park.

It seems unlikely that everyone was delighted.

Practice Questions

Read the texts below, and then answer the questions underneath each one.

WARHURST WINS AGAIN

Michael Warhurst, the Independent candidate for Gawesbury, has been elected for the third year in a row.

Mr Warhurst has been the best MP Gawesbury has ever seen. He campaigned against the closure of Gawesbury General Hospital and fought the opening of a new Metromarket supermarket which threatened businesses and shops in the town centre. Mr Warhurst will continue to campaign for the interests of the people of Gawesbury with all the locals' support.

---

1) Find **one** way the writer has tried to influence the reader's opinion from the text above. Support your answers with examples from the text.

Way the writer has tried to influence the reader ....

....

Example from the text..

....

---

http://www.beautyreviews.co.uk

beautyreviews.co.uk

Mane-tame Shampoo

Reviewed by Jane Ryan ☆☆☆☆☆

I'd heard good things about this shampoo so I bought a bottle last week, but sadly I was thoroughly disappointed. Not only was I absolutely outraged by the price, but the product itself smelt horrendous. Despite the hideous smell, I tried washing my hair with it this morning, but it made my hair greasier than a plate of chips. I will not be buying this shampoo again.

---

2) Find **two** ways the writer has tried to influence the reader's opinion from the text above. Support your answers with examples from the text.

First way the writer has tried to influence the reader...

....

Example from the text..

....

Second way the writer has tried to influence the reader...

....

Example from the text..

....

Spotting Different Types of Text

Letters and emails are sent to other people

1) Letters have **addresses**, a **date** and a **greeting** at the top, and a **sign-off** at the end.

2) Emails have a '**to**' and a '**from**' box at the top, as well as a box for the email's **subject**.

Adverts and leaflets try to grab your attention

1) Adverts are usually **persuasive**. They try to **convince** you to do something.

2) Leaflets are usually **informative**. They give you **information** about something.

3) Adverts and leaflets both use **colours**, **pictures** and different **fonts** to get **noticed**.

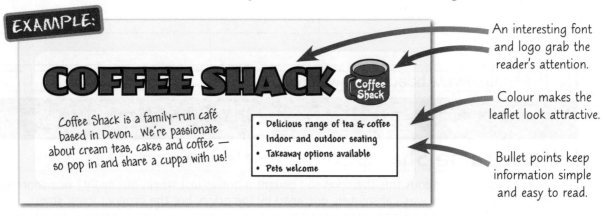

EXAMPLE:

An interesting font and logo grab the reader's attention.

Colour makes the leaflet look attractive.

Bullet points keep information simple and easy to read.

COFFEE SHACK

Coffee Shack is a family-run café based in Devon. We're passionate about cream teas, cakes and coffee — so pop in and share a cuppa with us!

- Delicious range of tea & coffee
- Indoor and outdoor seating
- Takeaway options available
- Pets welcome

Websites have specific features

They usually have an **address bar** at the top, a **search box** and **links** to other **web pages**.

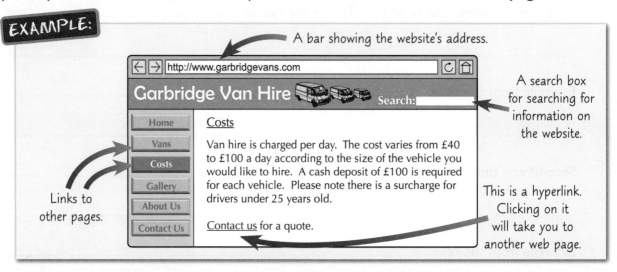

EXAMPLE:

A bar showing the website's address.

A search box for searching for information on the website.

http://www.garbridgevans.com

Garbridge Van Hire   Search:

Home
Vans
Costs
Gallery
About Us
Contact Us

Costs

Van hire is charged per day. The cost varies from £40 to £100 a day according to the size of the vehicle you would like to hire. A cash deposit of £100 is required for each vehicle. Please note there is a surcharge for drivers under 25 years old.

Contact us for a quote.

Links to other pages.

This is a hyperlink. Clicking on it will take you to another web page.

Spotting Different Types of Text

Articles are in newspapers or magazines

1) They have **headlines** to tell you what the article is **about**.

2) **Subheadings** and **columns** are used to break up the text.

Practice Questions

Look at the four text types below and then answer the questions underneath each one.

1) What type of text is this?

....

2) Name **one** feature that tells you this.

....

3) What type of text is this?

....

4) Name **one** feature that tells you this.

....

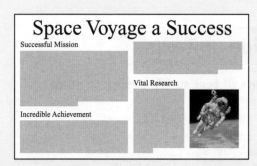

5) What type of text is this?

....

6) Name **one** feature that tells you this.

....

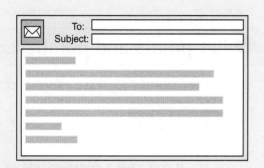

7) What type of text is this?

....

8) Name **one** feature that tells you this.

....

Spotting Presentational Features

Different texts have different presentational features

1) Texts can be **laid out** using different **features**, like **headlines, colours** and **bullet points**.

2) These are called **presentational features** and they make a text **easier to understand**.

Headlines and subheadings tell you what a text is about

1) **Headlines** and **titles** are always at the **top** of the page in a bigger font.

2) They try to **grab** the reader's **attention** and get them to read the text.

3) **Subheadings** tell you what a section of a text is about.

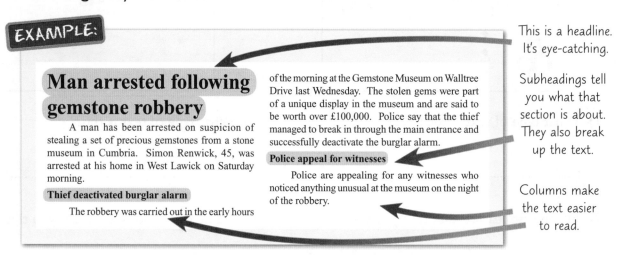

EXAMPLE:

Man arrested following gemstone robbery

A man has been arrested on suspicion of stealing a set of precious gemstones from a stone museum in Cumbria. Simon Renwick, 45, was arrested at his home in West Lawick on Saturday morning.

Thief deactivated burglar alarm

The robbery was carried out in the early hours of the morning at the Gemstone Museum on Walltree Drive last Wednesday. The stolen gems were part of a unique display in the museum and are said to be worth over £100,000. Police say that the thief managed to break in through the main entrance and successfully deactivate the burglar alarm.

Police appeal for witnesses

Police are appealing for any witnesses who noticed anything unusual at the museum on the night of the robbery.

This is a headline. It's eye-catching.

Subheadings tell you what that section is about. They also break up the text.

Columns make the text easier to read.

Bullet points and numbered lists divide up texts

1) **Bullet points** separate information into **short** bits of text so it's **easier** to **read**.

EXAMPLE:

If you have a question, please contact us by:
- Emailing us at ask@flixstationery.com
- Phoning us on 081360 876 543

Bullet points separate each piece of information. This makes the writing clear.

2) **Numbered lists** can be used instead of bullet points.

3) This is usually for things that are **in a set order**, such as a set of **instructions**.

Read the texts below, and then answer the questions underneath each one.

Ⓐ

Noah's bark to the rescue

By *Jamal Dove*

A pensioner's dog is being praised for bravery during last week's flooding at Low Bridge. The dog's barking attracted the attention of the fire service who came to rescue his owner, 72-year-old Mrs Wallace.

Dog barked in rain for three hours

Mrs Wallace was suffering from flu and was sleeping as the floodwaters rose around her house on Riverside Lane. When she woke, she was trapped upstairs. She tried to shout for help out of the window, but her voice was too quiet against the roar of the river. Her 8-year-old Labrador, Noah, climbed onto the windowsill and began to bark. After 2 hours firemen working nearby heard the dog and came to investigate. Noah stayed on the windowsill barking until Mrs Wallace was rescued by helicopter an hour later.

"I could have died if it wasn't for Noah."

Mrs Wallace was brought to Bridgedale Community Hospital where she was treated for shock. She said afterwards, "Noah was my saviour. I could have died if it wasn't for him".

Noah was cared for by a local animal shelter until he could be returned to Mrs Wallace.

Ⓑ

Ⓒ

1) a)   Name presentational feature A. ....

   b)   Give **one** reason why it is effective. ....

   ....

2) a)   Name presentational feature B. ....

   b)   Give **one** reason why it is effective. ....

   ....

3) a)   Name presentational feature C. ....

   b)   Give **one** reason why it is effective. ....

   ....

Ⓓ

There are a number of reasons why it's important to check your bank balance regularly:

• You will have a better idea how much money you are spending.

• You are less likely to go overdrawn on your account.

• You can make sure all your payments have gone through.

• If you are a victim of fraud, you will notice immediately.

4) a)   Name presentational feature D. ....

   b)   Give **one** reason why it is effective. ....

   ....

Spotting Presentational Features

Graphics and captions help you understand a text

A **graphic** is a **picture**, **diagram** or **chart**. It shows you what the text is about.

EXAMPLE:

Third Oil Spill Hits French Coastline

The third oil spill in four weeks has hit the north-west coast of France. The oil was released from a tanker which ran aground in the Atlantic, 30 miles offshore. Beaches along the coast have been closed to the public while the clean-up process takes place.

Volunteers clean a beach near Carnac after the spill.

The graphic shows people cleaning up the oil spill. It helps the reader imagine the situation.

Graphics also make the text more interesting to read.

A caption is a bit of text that tells you more about the graphic. It makes it clear what the graphic is about.

Colour affects how you read a text

1) Colourful **text** and **backgrounds** create an effect on the reader.

2) **Bright colours** make text look more **fun**.

3) **Dark colours** create a **serious mood** suitable for more **formal** texts.

Fonts help set the tone of a text

1) **Serious, formal** fonts are for **serious, formal** texts.

2) **Cartoony, childish** fonts are for **light-hearted** texts, or texts for **children**.

3) Some words might be highlighted in **bold** or in *italics* to make them **stand out**.

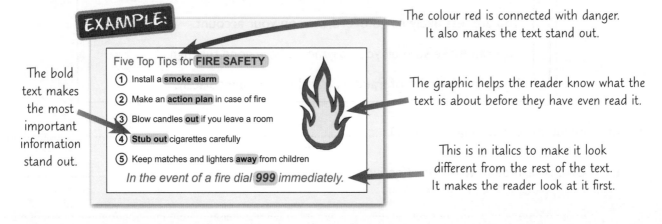

EXAMPLE:

Five Top Tips for **FIRE SAFETY**

① Install a **smoke alarm**

② Make an **action plan** in case of fire

③ Blow candles **out** if you leave a room

④ **Stub out** cigarettes carefully

⑤ Keep matches and lighters **away** from children

In the event of a fire dial **999** *immediately.*

The bold text makes the most important information stand out.

The colour red is connected with danger. It also makes the text stand out.

The graphic helps the reader know what the text is about before they have even read it.

This is in italics to make it look different from the rest of the text. It makes the reader look at it first.

Practice Questions

Look at the texts below and then answer the questions underneath each one.

Mr Clean

Great value carpet cleaning!

Mr Clean can remove **any mark** or **stain**.
Customer satisfaction guaranteed.

*"My carpets looked like new after Mr Clean had seen to them.
His service was reliable and great value for money."* Mrs Jones, Birtley.

Call **01313 877778** now for a quote.

£10 per hour!

1) The text marked A is in bold. Give **one** reason why this is effective.

....

....

2) Give **one** reason why the graphic marked B is effective.

....

....

3) The text marked C is in italics:

a) To make it blend with the rest of the text   c) To make it stand out

b) To show that it is informative   d) To show you what the text is about

HOMEWARE SALE — 50% OFF

At Fratton Homes, we've cut prices on everything in store.
It's your chance to grab a great bargain:

- 50% off all bedding
- 50% off kitchenware
- 40% off all curtains
- 35% off beds and mattresses

FRATTON HOMES

4) Identify **two** presentational features in this text.

Feature 1 ....

Feature 2 ....

5) Choose **one** and give **one** reason why it is effective

....

....

Spotting Language Techniques

Texts use different techniques to persuade the reader

1) A **direct address to the reader** is when it sounds as if the writer is **speaking directly** to the reader.

2) This makes the text seem more **personal**, which may help to **persuade** the reader.

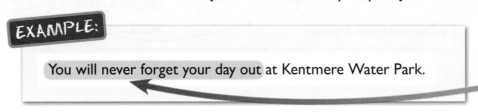

EXAMPLE:

You will never forget your day out at Kentmere Water Park.

Words such as 'you' and 'your' make it seem as though the text is addressing the reader personally.

3) **Rhetorical questions** are questions which don't need an **answer**.

4) They are used to try and persuade the reader to **agree** with the writer.

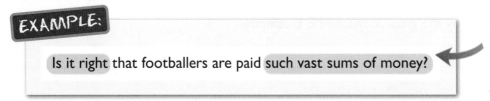

EXAMPLE:

Is it right that footballers are paid such vast sums of money?

The question is written so that the only sensible answer is 'no'. The writer is trying to make the reader agree with their point of view.

Adverts often use slogans to persuade the reader

1) Slogans are **short, memorable** phrases used in **advertising**.

2) **Alliteration** is used in slogans to make them **catchy** and easy to **remember**.

3) Alliteration is when words that are **close together** begin with the **same sound**.

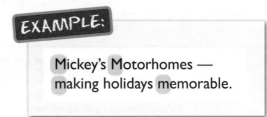

EXAMPLE:

Mickey's Motorhomes — making holidays memorable.

The 'rule of three' is used to create emphasis

1) The '**rule of three**' is when a writer uses a **list** of **three words** or **phrases** in their writing.

2) They do this to **emphasise** the point they are making.

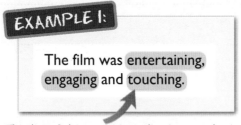

EXAMPLE 1:

The film was entertaining, engaging and touching.

This list of three positive adjectives emphasises the writer's positive feelings about the film.

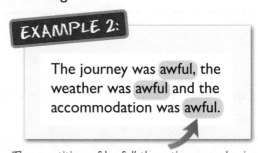

EXAMPLE 2:

The journey was awful, the weather was awful and the accommodation was awful.

The repetition of 'awful' three times emphasises the writer's negative feelings about their trip.

Practice Questions

Read the two texts below and then answer the questions underneath each one.

Yewbarrow Castle

Is there a better way to spend a day than exploring Yewbarrow Castle? With its impressive building, fascinating history and breathtaking surroundings, there is something for everyone to enjoy. The castle is full of surprises, including secret passages and hidden doors — who doesn't like getting lost now and again? Yewbarrow Castle is well worth a visit, and we want as many people as possible to experience our beautiful castle, its beautiful grounds and the beautiful landscape.

1) Which **two** persuasive techniques are used in this text?

    a)   Rule of three   c)   Rhetorical question

    b)   Direct address to the reader   d)   Alliteration

2) Give **one** example from the text of each technique.

....

....

BILLY'S BIKES
Builders of Beautiful Bikes

Here at Billy's Bikes, we specialise in creating your dream bike. If you have something special in mind, come and talk to us and we'll do our best to make it a reality. We just love the look on our customers' faces when they see their new bike for the first time!

We're also experts when it comes to sticky gears, squeaky brakes and rusty chains. So if you have any problems with your bike, bring it straight to us. We will do all we can to fix it for you. And don't forget, we're known across the country as Builders of Beautiful Bikes.

3) 'Builders of Beautiful Bikes' is an example of:

    a)   Rhetorical question   c)   Alliteration

    b)   Direct address to the reader   d)   Rule of three

4) Write down the names of **two** other language techniques used in the text.

....

....

Spotting Language Techniques

Similes and metaphors are used to describe things

1) Similes and metaphors help the reader to **imagine** what the writer is describing.

2) A **simile** is a way of describing something by **comparing** it to something else.

3) Similes often use words such as '**like**' or '**as**' to make comparisons.

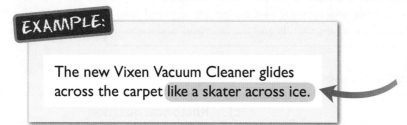

The new Vixen Vacuum Cleaner glides across the carpet like a skater across ice.

This simile compares the movement of the vacuum cleaner to someone skating over ice. This helps the reader imagine how easy the vacuum cleaner is to use.

4) A **metaphor** is a way of describing something by saying **it is** something else.

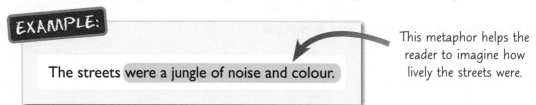

The streets were a jungle of noise and colour.

This metaphor helps the reader to imagine how lively the streets were.

Idioms are commonly used sayings

1) Idioms are phrases with a **set meaning** that is **different** from the **literal meaning** of the words.

2) For example, 'it's raining **cats and dogs**' is an idiom which means 'it's raining **heavily**'.

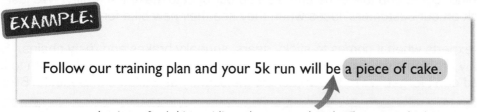

Follow our training plan and your 5k run will be a piece of cake.

'a piece of cake' is an idiom that means 'easy'. The writer thinks the run will be easy, not that it will literally be a piece of cake.

3) Writers use idioms to make their writing more **entertaining** and **interesting**.

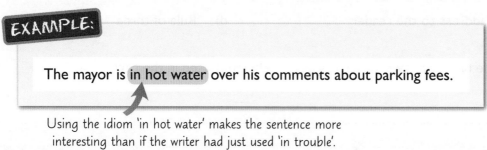

The mayor is in hot water over his comments about parking fees.

Using the idiom 'in hot water' makes the sentence more interesting than if the writer had just used 'in trouble'.

Practice Questions

1) Read each sentence and write next to each one whether it is a simile, a metaphor or an idiom.

    a) The hotel staff did whatever we asked at the drop of a hat. ....

    b) The stadium was a cauldron of nerves and anticipation. ....

    c) The film was as dull as a grey afternoon. ....

Read the text below and then answer the questions underneath.

← →   http://www.novelblog.books.org   ↻ ⌂

📖 **novelblog.books.org**

Take Fire to the Mountain

Tomorrow, Lee Nightingale's new novel *Take Fire to the Mountain* will finally be released, and I am on the edge of my seat. His last novel, published 16 years ago, had a huge impact on me — it was a tornado which hurtled into my life, changing it forever. As I wait for his new novel to drop through the letterbox, I feel like a child about to open their birthday presents. Nightingale is such a talented author — his novels transport me to another world. Waiting for a book to be released is like getting ready to set off on an adventure, and I have a feeling this is going to be a good one. In other good news, someone has let the cat out of the bag that Nightingale is working on another novel. How exciting!

2) 'it was a tornado which hurtled into my life' is an example of:

    a) A metaphor   c) A simile

    b) An idiom   d) A rhetorical question

3) How does the language technique in Question 2 help to express meaning?

    ....

    ....

4) Write down the meaning of the idiom 'let the cat out of the bag'.

    ....

5) Give **one** example of a simile from the text.

    ....

Identifying Tone and Style

Writing can have a personal or impersonal tone

1) **Personal** writing sounds like it is **talking to the reader**.

2) It's written from the writer's **point of view**, so it's full of **opinions** and it shows **emotion**.

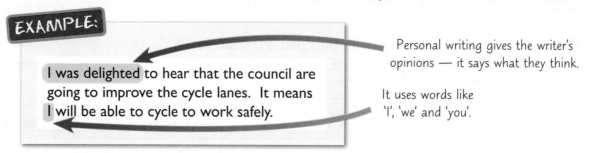

EXAMPLE:

I was delighted to hear that the council are going to improve the cycle lanes. It means I will be able to cycle to work safely.

Personal writing gives the writer's opinions — it says what they think.

It uses words like 'I', 'we' and 'you'.

3) **Impersonal** writing **doesn't** tell you anything about the writer's **personality**.

4) It just reports the **facts**, so it's usually **neutral** and doesn't take anybody's **side**.

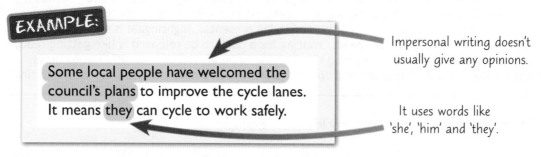

EXAMPLE:

Some local people have welcomed the council's plans to improve the cycle lanes. It means they can cycle to work safely.

Impersonal writing doesn't usually give any opinions.

It uses words like 'she', 'him' and 'they'.

Writing can have a formal or informal style

1) **Formal** writing sounds **serious**. It usually has an **impersonal tone**.

2) It is used for things like **job applications** because it **sounds** more **professional**.

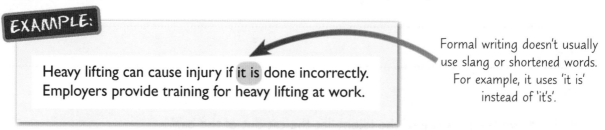

EXAMPLE:

Heavy lifting can cause injury if it is done incorrectly. Employers provide training for heavy lifting at work.

Formal writing doesn't usually use slang or shortened words. For example, it uses 'it is' instead of 'it's'.

3) **Informal** writing sounds **chatty**. It usually has a **personal tone**.

4) It is used for things like **letters** to your **family** because it's more **friendly**.

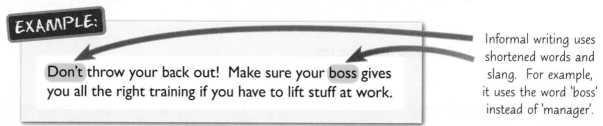

EXAMPLE:

Don't throw your back out! Make sure your boss gives you all the right training if you have to lift stuff at work.

Informal writing uses shortened words and slang. For example, it uses the word 'boss' instead of 'manager'.

Practice Questions

Read the text below, and then answer the questions underneath.

Dave and Tania are getting hitched!

Love is in the air

Dear ...Sanjay...

We're getting married on Saturday 14th July and we'd love you to come and celebrate with us.

Where: St John's in the Valley, Bridgeley

When: One o'clock

We want our wedding to be a really fun and relaxed day. The wedding reception is going to be in the church hall and we're going to have a bouncy castle and games to play outside. There'll be a barbecue and plenty of booze to go around. We'd like everyone to stay for the evening and dance their socks off.

Dress Code: Please come in whatever you feel most comfortable wearing. If you want to wear jeans, feel free.

Presents: We're going to Mauritius on our honeymoon. We'd be really grateful if you could contribute to our honeymoon fund.

Please let us know if you can come by emailing **daveandtania@wedding.co.uk**

1) a)   Is the tone of this invitation personal or impersonal? ....

    b)   How can you tell?

....

....

2) The text suggests that:

    a)   The wedding is going to be serious   c)   The dress code is very formal

    b)   The wedding is going to be casual   d)   The reception will only be held outside

3) a)   Is the style of this invitation formal or informal? ....

    b)   How can you tell?

....

....

4) Why do you think this style has been used?

    a)   To make Sanjay feel excited   c)   It matches the style of the wedding

    b)   It is a wedding invitation   d)   To give information clearly

Selecting Texts

Texts with different purposes can be about the same thing

1) Information can be presented in a lot of **different ways** and have **different purposes**.

2) Some texts could use the **same information**, but have a **different purpose**.

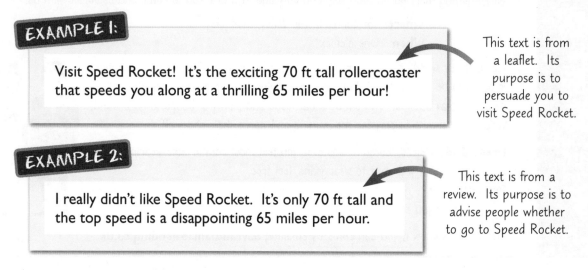

EXAMPLE 1:

Visit Speed Rocket! It's the exciting 70 ft tall rollercoaster that speeds you along at a thrilling 65 miles per hour!

This text is from a leaflet. Its purpose is to persuade you to visit Speed Rocket.

EXAMPLE 2:

I really didn't like Speed Rocket. It's only 70 ft tall and the top speed is a disappointing 65 miles per hour.

This text is from a review. Its purpose is to advise people whether to go to Speed Rocket.

Pick the most useful source

1) When you're looking for information, **don't** just pick the **first source** you can find.

2) Make sure you pick the source that **best suits** your **needs**.

3) Sometimes you'll need to look at **more than one source** to find what you need.

EXAMPLE:

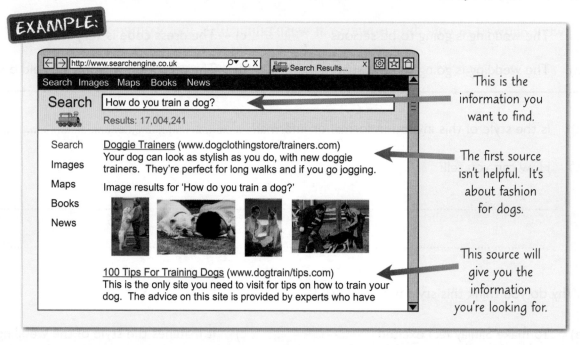

http://www.searchengine.co.uk	Search Results...

Search   Images   Maps   Books   News

Search   How do you train a dog?

Results: 17,004,241

Search

Images

Maps

Books

News

Doggie Trainers (www.dogclothingstore/trainers.com)
Your dog can look as stylish as you do, with new doggie trainers. They're perfect for long walks and if you go jogging.

Image results for 'How do you train a dog?'

100 Tips For Training Dogs (www.dogtrain/tips.com)
This is the only site you need to visit for tips on how to train your dog. The advice on this site is provided by experts who have

This is the information you want to find.

The first source isn't helpful. It's about fashion for dogs.

This source will give you the information you're looking for.

Read the texts below, and then answer the questions underneath.

Source A

VOTE FOR THE ECO-FRIENDLY PARTY

If elected, the Eco-Friendly party aims to:

- **build a brand-new recycling centre**

- **provide each house with recycling boxes for glass and paper**

- **campaign against the proposals for the new airport**

Source B

How do I register to vote?

search 🔍

There are several ways you can register to vote. Here's how:

1) <u>Fill in the electronic form below</u> and we'll send you a voting pack in the post. You'll then need to sign a form and post it back to us.

2) <u>Call 01111 232345</u> and give us your details. We'll send you a voting pack in the post, then you'll need to fill in some forms and return them to us.

Source C

The History of Voting

Nowadays, everyone over the age of 18 has the right to vote, but it's not always been that way. In the 1400s, only rich people were allowed to vote. By the mid-1800s, most men from cities were given the right to vote, and in 1884, men from the countryside were allowed to vote too. However, it wasn't until 1918, that women were able to vote, and even then they had to be over thirty years old. Eventually, in 1969, the age limit for voting was lowered to 18 years old for both men and women.

1) You're writing a report about different political parties. Which source would be most helpful?

   Source ....

2) You want to find out about voting in the nineteenth century. Which source would you choose?

   Source ....

3) You're giving a presentation telling people how to vote. Which source would be most helpful?

   Source ....

Picking Out the Main Points

Scan the text to work out the main points

1) You **don't** need to read the **whole text** to find the **main points**.

2) Move your eyes **quickly** over the text, looking for **key words**.

3) **Key words** are things that tell you **who, what, where, when, why** and **how**.

4) **Underline** any key words that you find.

EXAMPLE 1:

<u>Lions</u> usually <u>live</u> in a <u>family group, which is called a pride</u>. A pride is often made up of <u>one adult male lion</u> and <u>up to six adult female lions</u>.

The main points from the text are underlined. This tells you what the text is about.

EXAMPLE 2:

The <u>New Forest Adventure Park</u> is <u>an adventure playground for children</u>. It is located in the <u>heart of the New Forest</u>, just off the M27. The park has a <u>15 ft slide</u>, a <u>climbing wall</u> and a <u>giant rope swing</u>.

The key words tell you that the text is informing the reader about the Adventure Park.

The most important point usually comes first

1) Each **paragraph** in a text has its **own main point**.

2) The **most important point** is usually in the **first paragraph**.

EXAMPLE:

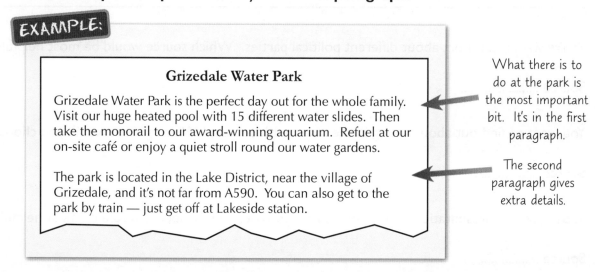

Grizedale Water Park

Grizedale Water Park is the perfect day out for the whole family. Visit our huge heated pool with 15 different water slides. Then take the monorail to our award-winning aquarium. Refuel at our on-site café or enjoy a quiet stroll round our water gardens.

The park is located in the Lake District, near the village of Grizedale, and it's not far from A590. You can also get to the park by train — just get off at Lakeside station.

What there is to do at the park is the most important bit. It's in the first paragraph.

The second paragraph gives extra details.

Practice Questions

Read the text below, and then answer the questions underneath.

Caring For Your Horse.com

	You are here: Home > Feeding	Search:
Home		
Feeding		
Grooming		
Hoof Care		
Illness		
FAQs		
Forum		

You are here: Home > Feeding

Feeding a Horse

A horse's natural diet includes grass, herbs and weeds. You should give your horse hay in winter when there's less fresh grass in the fields. You can also buy 'feed' (special food) which has the vitamins, proteins and carbohydrates that horses need.

If you take your horse on a long ride, or compete in events that use a lot of energy like show jumping, you should provide it with high-energy food. Oats and barley will provide an active horse with plenty of energy, but too much might make your horse overweight.

Watering a Horse

A horse can drink between 30 and 50 litres of water each day. You need to make sure your horse has plenty of clean water. Keep a plastic bucket in your horse's stable to give it something to drink from. Make sure you change the water regularly and keep the bucket clean. Your horse will also need a water trough in its field.

1) The **main** purpose of this text is:

   a) To tell the reader how to groom horses   c) To persuade the reader to buy a horse

   b) To tell the reader about a horses diet   d) To tell the reader how to ride a horse

2) According to the text, name **one** thing that is part of the natural diet of a horse.

....

3) According to the text, what should you feed a horse to give it more energy?

   a) Grass   c) 'Feed'

   b) Water   d) Oats

4) According to the text, why should you keep a plastic bucket in your horse's stable?

....

5) According to the text, what does a horse need in winter?

....

Reading for Detail

The layout of a text can help you find details

1) **Presentational features** like titles and subheadings tell you **where** to find information.

2) Use them to decide which **part** of a text to **check first**.

3) Then **scan** that part of the text to find the **details** you're looking for.

EXAMPLE:

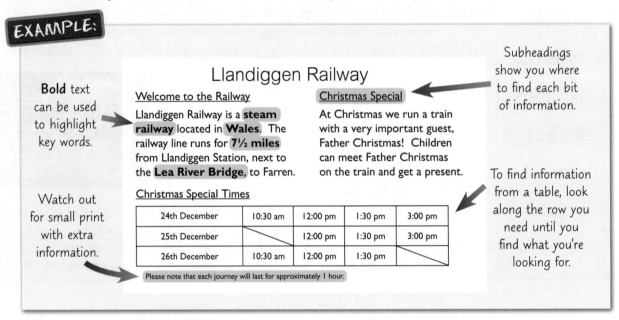

Bold text can be used to highlight key words.

Watch out for small print with extra information.

Llandiggen Railway

Welcome to the Railway

Llandiggen Railway is a **steam railway** located in **Wales**. The railway line runs for **7½ miles** from Llandiggen Station, next to the **Lea River Bridge**, to Farren.

Christmas Special

At Christmas we run a train with a very important guest, Father Christmas! Children can meet Father Christmas on the train and get a present.

Christmas Special Times

24th December	10:30 am	12:00 pm	1:30 pm	3:00 pm
25th December		12:00 pm	1:30 pm	3:00 pm
26th December	10:30 am	12:00 pm	1:30 pm	

Please note that each journey will last for approximately 1 hour.

Subheadings show you where to find each bit of information.

To find information from a table, look along the row you need until you find what you're looking for.

The information you need can be tricky to find

The **information** you **need** from a text might be in things like **graphs**, **charts** and **tables**.

EXAMPLE:

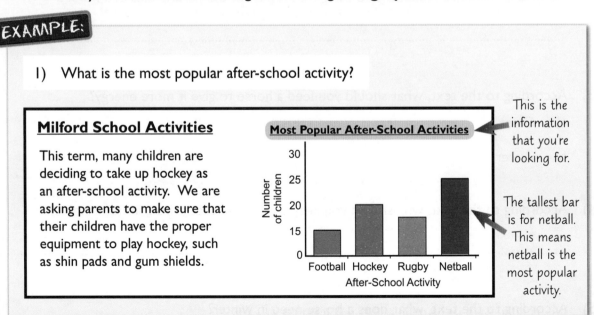

1) What is the most popular after-school activity?

Milford School Activities

This term, many children are deciding to take up hockey as an after-school activity. We are asking parents to make sure that their children have the proper equipment to play hockey, such as shin pads and gum shields.

Most Popular After-School Activities

This is the information that you're looking for.

The tallest bar is for netball. This means netball is the most popular activity.

Read the text below, and then answer the questions underneath.

Massive Furniture Sale!

At Furnish Plus, we've gone sale crazy and slashed the prices on all our leading ranges. But you'll have to hurry. These amazing sale prices will only be available on April 28th.

Great Deals

Just look at some of the extraordinary deals on furniture you can get at Furnish Plus:

Item	WAS	NOW	SAVING
Standford Office Desk	£149.99	£99.99	33%
McIntyre Classic Dresser	£899.99	£599.99	33%
Brockwell 3-seater Sofa	£750.00	£375.00	50%

Easy to Find

There are loads more offers in the store. Come down and have a look for yourself. You'll find us at 48 Morley Road, Smithsgate Retail Park. Get here early to avoid the queues!

Comfee Armchairs Only £99!

1) When is the sale being held?

....

2) Where is Furnish Plus?

....

3) Which item of furniture is the most expensive after the discount?

a) Standford Office Desk   c) Comfee Armchair

b) Brockwell 3-seater Sofa   d) McIntyre Classic Dresser

4) How much did the Brockwell 3-seater Sofa cost before the discount?

a) £149.99   c) £750.00

b) £99   d) £899.99

5) Name **one** item of furniture that has a saving of 33%.

....

Using Information

A summary is a brief description of the important points

1) A summary sometimes comes at the **start** a text, for example in an article.

2) It introduces the **important points**.

> EXAMPLE:
>
> This article is about physical education in schools and its importance to children's health. It will also look at how physical education teaches children about teamwork and cooperation, which are skills that everyone needs.
>
> These are the most important points in the text.

3) A summary sometimes comes at the **end** of a text, for example in a report.

4) It can **sum up** an argument and give the writer's **opinion**.

> EXAMPLE:
>
> Opening a new library will mean that we will all have to pay more council tax to fund it. However, the educational benefit of the library will be good for everyone. That is why I think it would be an excellent idea to open a new library.
>
> The first two sentences summarise the main points.
>
> The last sentence gives an opinion.

A text might require you to respond to something

1) Different texts will require you to **respond** in **different ways**.

2) A text might ask for you to **write a comment** or **confirm something**.

3) Others might ask you to **call** a **phone number**, **write** to an **address** or **visit** a **website**.

> EXAMPLE:
>
> 8) How can you find more information about adopting an orangutan?
>
> For just £5 a month you can adopt an orangutan and help pay for the food needed at the orangutan's sanctuary. To find out more about adopting an orangutan, please go to our website www.orangutansanctuary.my.org.
>
> You need to visit the website to find out more information about adopting an orangutan.

Practice Questions

Read the text below, and then answer the questions underneath.

Fury Over New Housing

Hendley Council have given their support to controversial plans for a new luxury housing estate. This has caused outrage among the residents of Hendley.

The London firm Hythes Housing will build the multi-million pound estate on the site of the derelict playground near to St Paul's churchyard. Local residents had hoped that this site would be used for a new children's play area.

When the decision was announced, about thirty people gathered outside the council offices and jeered at the councillors when they emerged. The protests were led by Greg Fisher. He said, "This is a disgraceful decision. Money has won out over the genuine needs of local people. The new play area is desperately needed for the borough's children." Mr Fisher went on to claim that the councillors had "dollar signs in their eyes".

Councillor Carol Swann responded, "We know that feelings are running high over this issue, but we are confident we can reach a solution that is acceptable to everyone." She described the development as an "exciting new scheme" from which "everyone will benefit, including local people."

If you would like to have your say on this issue, please visit our forum at www.hendleyissues.forum.

1) Who is going to build the new luxury housing estate?

   a)   Hendley Council   c)   Greg Fisher

   b)   Hythes Housing   d)   Carol Swann

2) Where in Hendley will the new housing estate be built?

   ....

3) How can you give your own opinion on the new housing estate?

   ....

4) What does Greg Fisher think should be built instead of the new housing estate?

   ....

5) Write down **two** things that Carol Swann said about the new housing estate.

   1. ....

   2. ....

Using More Than One Text

You might need to use more than one source

1) One source may **not** give you all the information that you need.

2) Sometimes you'll have to use **another source** to get **all** of the **information**.

EXAMPLE:

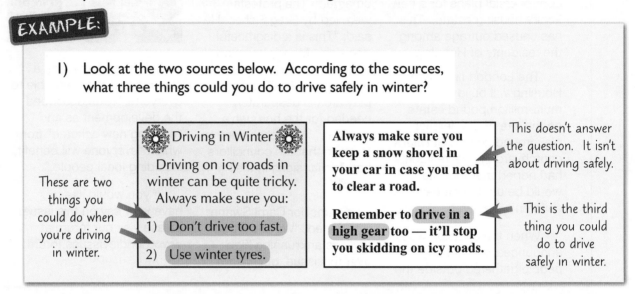

1) Look at the two sources below. According to the sources, what three things could you do to drive safely in winter?

❄ Driving in Winter ❄

Driving on icy roads in winter can be quite tricky. Always make sure you:

1) Don't drive too fast.

2) Use winter tyres.

These are two things you could do when you're driving in winter.

Always make sure you keep a snow shovel in your car in case you need to clear a road.

Remember to drive in a high gear too — it'll stop you skidding on icy roads.

This doesn't answer the question. It isn't about driving safely.

This is the third thing you could do to drive safely in winter.

Look for similarities and differences between texts

1) When you're **comparing two texts**, look for the ways that they are **similar**...

2) ...and the ways that they are **different**.

3) You might need to decide which text is **more suitable** for a particular **audience**.

EXAMPLE:

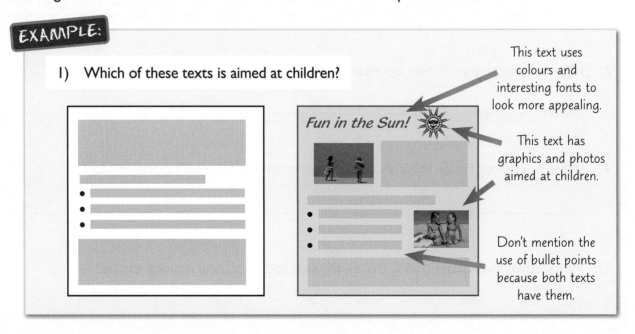

1) Which of these texts is aimed at children?

Fun in the Sun! ☀

This text uses colours and interesting fonts to look more appealing.

This text has graphics and photos aimed at children.

Don't mention the use of bullet points because both texts have them.

Read the texts below, and then answer the questions underneath.

Source A

Exercise for Life

Exercise is one of the best ways to stay healthy. Here are some easy ways to add more exercise to your daily routine:

- If you get a lunch hour at work, try and leave your office for a quick power walk. Not only will this provide you with some exercise, but the fresh air will make you feel more alert.

- In the summer, when it's light in the evenings, try to get out for a quick jog before dinner.

- In winter it can be harder to get out and about, so why not buy a workout DVD that you can do in the comfort of your own home?

Source B

I BEING HEALTHY

Looking after your heart is really important.

Here are some ways to make sure your heart is fighting fit:

- Sport is really good for keeping your heart strong — try joining a sports club.

- Don't eat too much junk food because this can damage your heart. Instead eat lots of fruit and vegetables to keep your heart fit.

- If you're usually driven to school, ask your parents if you can walk instead. Even if you only walk to school once a week, it will help protect your heart, as well as the environment!

1) Which source is more suitable for children?

   Source ....

2) You are making a leaflet about keeping fit and healthy. Using both **Source A** and **Source B**, select four ways someone could add more exercise into their daily routine.

   1. ....
   ....
   2. ....
   ....
   3. ....
   ....
   4. ....
   ....

Different Types of Question

There's only one correct answer for multiple-choice questions

1) In multiple-choice questions you'll be given a **right** answer and some **wrong** ones.

2) You have to choose the **correct option**.

3) **Rule out** the **options** that are **definitely wrong** until you're left with the **right answer**.

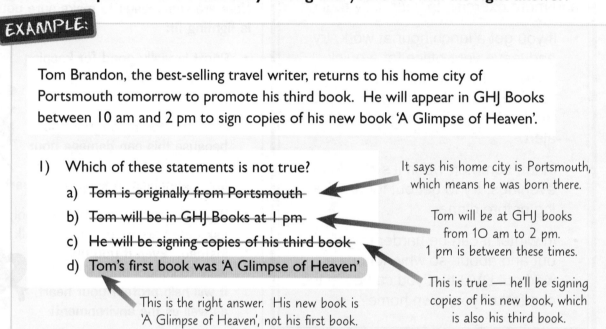

EXAMPLE:

Tom Brandon, the best-selling travel writer, returns to his home city of Portsmouth tomorrow to promote his third book. He will appear in GHJ Books between 10 am and 2 pm to sign copies of his new book 'A Glimpse of Heaven'.

1) Which of these statements is not true?
   a) ~~Tom is originally from Portsmouth~~
   b) ~~Tom will be in GHJ Books at 1 pm~~
   c) ~~He will be signing copies of his third book~~
   d) Tom's first book was 'A Glimpse of Heaven'

It says his home city is Portsmouth, which means he was born there.

Tom will be at GHJ books from 10 am to 2 pm. 1 pm is between these times.

This is true — he'll be signing copies of his new book, which is also his third book.

This is the right answer. His new book is 'A Glimpse of Heaven', not his first book.

Sometimes you'll have to write out your answer

1) Questions which **aren't multiple choice** will have a **space** for you to write your answer.

2) Make sure you **write enough** to answer the question **properly**.

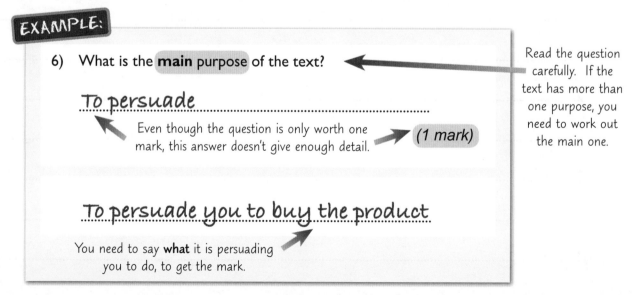

EXAMPLE:

6) What is the **main** purpose of the text?

To persuade
(1 mark)

Even though the question is only worth one mark, this answer doesn't give enough detail.

Read the question carefully. If the text has more than one purpose, you need to work out the main one.

To persuade you to buy the product

You need to say **what** it is persuading you to do, to get the mark.

Different Types of Question

Sometimes it won't be clear how much you need to write

1) Some longer questions might **not** tell you **how much** to write.

2) Use the **number of marks** available to work out how much to write.

EXAMPLE:

15) You have been asked to write a report about sports facilities in your area. Choose information and ideas from **Source B** that you might use in your report.

There are weekly swimming classes

There are local five-a-side football teams

Gyms offer 2 months free membership

There is one-to-one coaching available

(4 marks)

Only use Source B to answer the question. You won't get any marks for including ideas from elsewhere.

The question doesn't tell you how much to write...

...but it's worth four marks, so you should write four points.

Sometimes you have to give a reason to support your answer

1) Some questions will expect you to **find** the answer from the **source**.

2) Other questions will expect you to **use** your **own knowledge**.

EXAMPLE:

16) Reread **Sources A** and **B**. Decide which of the texts uses presentational features more effectively and say why. Give **two** examples to support your answer.

The most effective Source is ......A......

Presentational feature 1 and a reason why it is effective:

Italics for subheadings make them stand out

Presentational feature 2 and a reason why it is effective:

The graph backs up the ideas in the text

This is the presentational feature.

This is the reason.

(4 marks)

You have to think of your own reason **why** each presentational feature is effective to get all four marks.

Practice Questions

Read **Source A** below, and then answer the questions underneath.

Whatever sport you do, whether it's running, football or swimming, it's likely that you will pick up an injury at some point. By visiting a professional sports physio like me, you can make sure that you'll get fighting fit as soon as possible.

I specialise in dealing with:

- **Strains and sprains** — two of the most common sports injuries. I can help you with any discomfort and speed up the healing process.

- **Back and neck pain** — using a combination of hot and cold compresses, I can loosen up your muscles with a high-intensity shoulder, neck and head rub.

- **Joint pain and arthritis** — I have lots of experience treating elderly clients and I have designed a special fitness programme so you can keep trim even with reduced movement.

I also offer sports massages, ideal for warming down after a hard workout session.

I am fully-trained with 10 years experience as a physio. I offer professionalism at a very affordable price. Contact me at *Mark.Pitt@sportsphysio.org* or on *05448 221111* for a <u>free quote</u> or for <u>more information</u>.

1) According to the information in the text, which of these statements is true?

    a) Sports massages are good for joint pain   c) You can contact Mark Pitt by post

    b) You might get injured swimming   d) Arthritis stops you exercising

2) What is the **main** purpose of this text?

....

....

3) Give **two** examples of presentational features from **Source A**, and give a reason why each feature is effective.

Presentational feature 1 and a reason why it is effective:

....

....

Presentational feature 2 and a reason why it is effective:

....

....

Reading Test Advice

You're not marked on spelling, punctuation or grammar

1) In the **reading test** you **don't** need to worry about **spelling, punctuation** or **grammar**...

2) ... but if you need to copy out **quotes** from the **source**, make sure you spell them **correctly**.

3) Don't use your **dictionary** too much. Only use it if it will help you **answer** a question.

4) Answers **don't** have to be in **sentences**, but make sure you answer the **question** fully.

5) Make sure you've picked out the **correct information** and that your answer is **clear**.

Read every question carefully

The most important thing to remember is to:

Make sure you **answer the question**. Only pick out **relevant information**.

1) Check each question to make sure you're using the **correct source**.

2) This is especially important if you're **comparing two sources**.

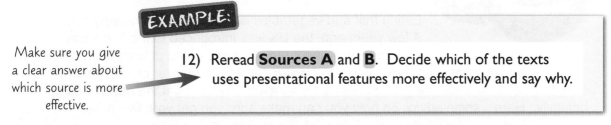

EXAMPLE:

Make sure you give a clear answer about which source is more effective.

12) Reread **Sources A** and **B**. Decide which of the texts uses presentational features more effectively and say why.

3) Use your **time sensibly**. Spend **more time** on questions worth **more marks**.

4) If you're stuck on a **multiple-choice question**, make a **sensible guess**.

5) Make sure **each point** you write is **separate** and you haven't put the **same thing twice**.

Prepare well for onscreen testing

1) If you're doing your test on a computer, try out the **onscreen sample test** beforehand.

2) Make sure you know what all the **buttons** do and how the test **works**.

3) At the start of the real test there will be a **tutorial** explaining how to answer each question type.

4) Ask your **tutor** for **more information** about what your test will be like.

Reading Test I

Give yourself **50 minutes** to do this test.

For multiple-choice questions, circle the letter you have chosen.
For longer answer questions, write your answers in the space provided.
You do not have to write in full sentences. You may use a dictionary.

Read **Source A** and answer questions 1-4.

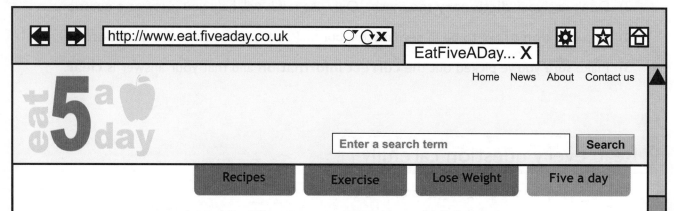

Getting your five a day

With obesity rates rising to alarming levels in the UK, people are being encouraged to take a look at their lifestyle choices. People are having to think more carefully about what they are eating and how it's affecting their health.

Eating fruit and vegetables is important for a healthy diet. A few years ago, the UK was introduced to the five a day scheme which encourages people to eat at least five portions of fruit and vegetables a day. According to *Health-CC*, only a quarter of adults meet this daily target. As a result, the government is trying even harder to get the nation eating healthily. Here's some advice on how you can make sure you get your five a day:

- Porridge is a great way to start the day, but adding a handful of **fresh berries** or some **chopped fruit** makes it even healthier. This would make it count as one of your five a day.

- Add a glass of **fruit juice** to your breakfast and you're already ticking off another one of your five a day. One 150 ml glass of fresh juice with your breakfast will quench your thirst and help keep you healthy.

- **Carrot sticks** and a low-fat dip can be a tasty alternative when you need a quick snack, and they will provide you with more vitamins than a bar of chocolate.

- If you're not keen on vegetables, try **finely chopping peppers** and **carrots** before adding them to sauces, like bolognese, for example. This means you won't even notice you're eating another of your five a day.

People have reported that by making these small changes to their diet they sleep better, have clearer skin, more energy and can concentrate more — so there's no reason why you shouldn't start eating more healthily today!

1) The **main** purpose of the web page is to:

    a)   Tell you to completely change your diet   c)   Inform you how to eat more healthily

    b)   Explain the problems about obesity   d)   Tell you about Health-CC's campaigns

(1 mark)

2) What does the web page inform you about the lifestyles that people lead in the UK?

....

....

....

....

(2 marks)

3) Using **Source A**, identify **three** ways in which someone could ensure they eat more fruit and vegetables.

....

....

....

....

(3 marks)

4) Using **Source A**, identify **two** benefits of eating more healthily.

    1 ....

    2 ....

(2 marks)

Read **Source B** and answer questions 5-9.

Would you risk your health to diet?

Health*Extra*

MANY celebrities use extreme crash diets to lose weight quickly before photoshoots or red carpet events. Although these diets can have rapid results, they can also have dangerous effects on a person's health. Worryingly, more and more people are following in the footsteps of celebrities and are turning to crash diets to help them lose weight. Here are some of the most popular crash diets around:

People on the **Lemonade Diet** drink a salt-water drink when they wake up and then a lemonade mixture throughout the rest of the day. Dieters have been known to stay on this diet for over 10 days and can lose up to two pounds a day.

Dieters on the **Hollywood Diet** consume a special energy drink made of natural juices and essential vitamins for 48 hours and often lose up to five pounds in one day.

Cabbage Soup dieters live off cabbage soup and water for an entire week and can lose up to ten pounds during this time.

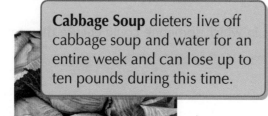

People who put themselves on these diets appear to lose weight at an astonishing speed, but at what cost?

Consuming such a low number of calories a day drastically reduces how much energy we have and therefore reduces concentration levels — crash dieters often experience shakiness and even memory loss. Not only does consuming just one type of food or drink get repetitive, but it can cause all sorts of health problems. Malnutrition is one of them — a single energy drink cannot possibly provide all the essential vitamins and minerals that a healthy balanced diet would provide.

So, if you want to lose weight without the dangerous side-effects, it's probably best to ignore the celebrities and stick to a healthy balanced diet and regular exercise.

Next week: Health*Extra* investigates... **Superfoods**

5) Identify the **main** purpose of the article and give supporting evidence from Source B.

....

....

(2 marks)

6) Give **one** quotation from Source B that suggests that crash diets can be bad for your health.

....

....

(1 mark)

7) 'Would you risk your health to diet?' is an example of:

a) the rule of three   c) a rhetorical question

b) a simile   d) alliteration

(1 mark)

8) Identify **two** layout features of **Source B** that help convey the information.

....

....

....

....

(2 marks)

9) Identify **two** problems associated with crash diets.

1 ....

2 ....

(2 marks)

44

Read **Source C** and answer questions 10-12.

Gym 1

Weight-loss Workouts

The first step towards a healthy new you

Eaten too much over the Christmas period? Feeling unfit? Want to look good for summer? Make it your New Year's resolution to call Weight-loss Workouts! At Weight-loss Workouts our staff are trained to help people slim healthily and sensibly. We have lots of facilities including a fully-equipped gym, swimming pool, sauna, steam room and whirlpool bath. We can provide a personal diet and exercise programme to help you reach the weight you want.

For a free brochure or to find out about our great deals, please call 01764 553777.

Gym 2

TARGET CENTRAL

Our number one goal at Target Central is training you to the standard you want.

We tailor all our programmes to suit the individual and have specially trained coaches who will make sure you reach your fitness target.

So whether you're training for a marathon or just a 5k run, we've got the expertise to help.

"The Target Central team are great. I was training for the Great North Cycle and they made me work really hard. It all paid off — I came 1st!"
(James Smith)

Visit our website: www.targetcentral.co.uk and find out more about prices and timetables

Gym 3

Great Value Gym
Memberships available for everyone:
- Juniors & students £60/year
- Adults £80/year

Membership includes use of all our facilities:
- Gym
- Swimming pool
- 4 squash courts

Opening times:
- Monday – Friday: 9am – 7pm
- Weekends:10am – 4pm

Fitness classes also available on:
- Mondays at 3pm
- Saturdays at 11am

Please call 015634 323232 for more details and for availability of classes.

Reading Test Practice

10) The **main** purpose of the texts in **Source C** is to:

    a)   Tell you about weight-loss plans

    b)   Persuade you to join one of the gyms

    c)   Tell you how to train for a triathlon

    d)   Inform you about gym timetables

(1 mark)

11) A family member is taking part in a triathlon next year and needs some help with his training.
He mostly needs help with running and cycling but isn't sure how to progress.
Give the number of the gym you would recommend and explain your choice.

Gym ....

Explanation

....

....

(2 marks)

12) Based on the information in **Source C**, which gym would you choose?
Give **three** reasons. Don't forget — your reasons must refer **only** to the option you choose.

Gym ....

Reason 1

....

....

Reason 2

....

....

Reason 3

....

....

(3 marks)

Reading Test 2

Give yourself **50 minutes** to do this test.

For multiple-choice questions, circle the letter you have chosen.
For longer answer questions, write your answers in the space provided.
You do not have to write in full sentences. You may use a dictionary.

Read **Source A** and answer questions 1-4.

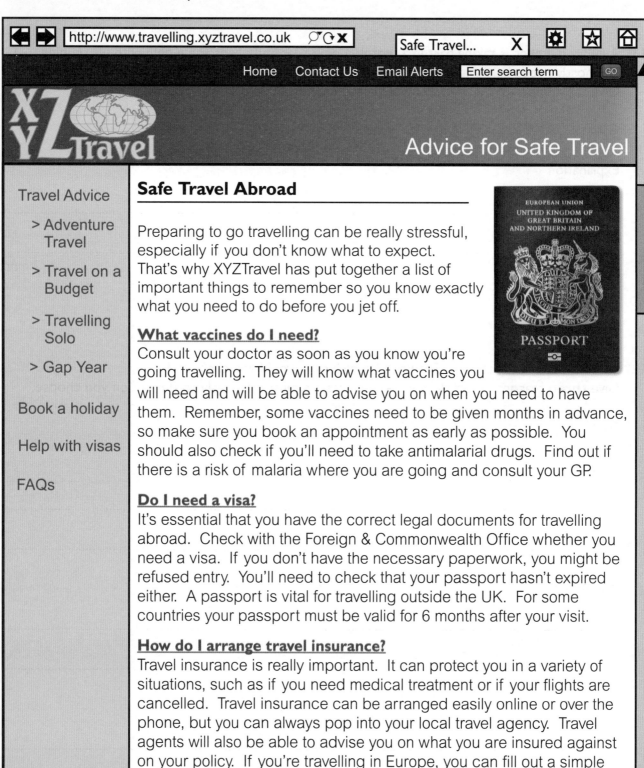

http://www.travelling.xyztravel.co.uk

Safe Travel...

Home   Contact Us   Email Alerts   Enter search term   GO

XYZTravel

Advice for Safe Travel

Travel Advice

> Adventure
  Travel

> Travel on a
  Budget

> Travelling
  Solo

> Gap Year

Book a holiday

Help with visas

FAQs

Safe Travel Abroad

Preparing to go travelling can be really stressful, especially if you don't know what to expect. That's why XYZTravel has put together a list of important things to remember so you know exactly what you need to do before you jet off.

What vaccines do I need?
Consult your doctor as soon as you know you're going travelling. They will know what vaccines you will need and will be able to advise you on when you need to have them. Remember, some vaccines need to be given months in advance, so make sure you book an appointment as early as possible. You should also check if you'll need to take antimalarial drugs. Find out if there is a risk of malaria where you are going and consult your GP.

Do I need a visa?
It's essential that you have the correct legal documents for travelling abroad. Check with the Foreign & Commonwealth Office whether you need a visa. If you don't have the necessary paperwork, you might be refused entry. You'll need to check that your passport hasn't expired either. A passport is vital for travelling outside the UK. For some countries your passport must be valid for 6 months after your visit.

How do I arrange travel insurance?
Travel insurance is really important. It can protect you in a variety of situations, such as if you need medical treatment or if your flights are cancelled. Travel insurance can be arranged easily online or over the phone, but you can always pop into your local travel agency. Travel agents will also be able to advise you on what you are insured against on your policy. If you're travelling in Europe, you can fill out a simple EHIC (European Health Insurance Card) form, for free. With an EHIC you can receive medical treatment abroad at a reduced price.

1) What does the website inform you about EHIC cards?

....

....

(1 mark)

2) The website suggests that:

    a)   It's difficult to get travel insurance   c)   You should prepare for your trip well

    b)   Vaccines aren't necessary   d)   Antimalarial drugs are expensive

(1 mark)

3) Explain why the picture has been used in **Source A**.

....

....

(1 mark)

4) Some texts have several different purposes, for example, to advise, to inform, to describe, to argue or to persuade.
Identify **two** purposes that **Source A** has and choose some text to support your answer.

1st purpose ....

Supporting text ....

....

....

2nd purpose ....

Supporting text ....

....

....

(4 marks)

Read **Source B** and answer questions 5-9.

Carbon Emissions

Long-haul flights v. carbon footprints

Nowadays, most people do their bit to protect the environment. Recycling has become part of daily life and lots of big supermarkets have on-site recycling facilities for their shoppers to use. Some people make an effort to walk or cycle short distances rather than using the car. Others even use eco-friendly resources, such as solar panels, to power their homes. These panels are an environmentally-friendly alternative to using coal and gas because they don't release harmful chemicals into the air. So it's hard to believe that a lot of people still take regular long-haul flights, even though they know that this method of travel is severely harming the environment.

Long-haul flights (flights longer than six hours) are popular because they are the quickest way of getting to far-flung places. But this convenient way of travelling is costing the planet dearly. Not only does

the amount of carbon released into the atmosphere increase with every extra mile travelled (making long-haul flights particularly damaging), but releasing carbon high up in the sky is even more harmful than releasing the same quantity at a lower level. Every year, around 700 million tonnes of carbon emissions are released into the atmosphere — and just from planes! And with people travelling more and more, and further and further away from home, the situation is only going to get worse. Carbon emission figures have almost doubled in the last ten years and are set to rise even higher.

Experts say that in the future, planes might run off cleaner fuels that create less pollution and therefore are less harmful to the planet. But until then, we must learn to live with the guilt of damaging the environment, or go on holiday closer to home.

Carbon emissions released from planes

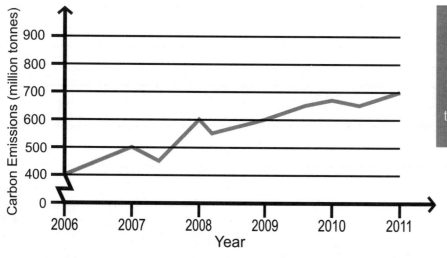

For more information about carbon emissions or to calculate your carbon footprint, visit our website: www. tellmemycarbonfootprint. co.uk

5) The article informs you that:

    a)   Long-haul flights are longer than 3 hours   c)   Carbon emissions have tripled recently

    b)   Long-haul flights are harming the planet   d)   Few people care about the environment

(1 mark)

6) The graph shows that carbon emissions:

    a)   Dropped between 2009-2010   c)   Rose by 100m tonnes during 2006-2007

    b)   Doubled between 2007-2008   d)   Decreased in 2009

(1 mark)

7) What does the article suggest about carbon emission figures in the future?

....

....

(1 mark)

8) Using **Source B**, identify **one** way the writer tries to influence the reader and give **one** example from the text.

Way: ....

....

Example:..

....

....

(2 marks)

9) **Source B** says that most people are making an effort to protect the environment. From the article, identify ways that people already care for the environment.

....

....

....

....

(3 marks)

Read **Source C** and answer questions 10-11.

SSAC

Sun Safety Awareness Campaign

STAY SAFE THIS SUMMER

Whether you're going on holiday somewhere hot or just relaxing in your garden, taking precautions against the sun's harmful rays is essential for healthy living. Take a look at these top tips to make sure you stay safe this summer.

Apply sun cream

Sun cream helps protect you against the sun's harmful UVA and UVB rays, which cause sunburn. Sun creams come with different sun protection factors (SPF), so make sure you choose the one that will give you sufficient protection. The higher the SPF, the more protection you'll get. Don't forget to reapply sun cream after swimming, even if the bottle says it's 'waterproof'.

Stay hydrated

Make sure you drink plenty of fluids, ideally water, when it's hot. This is important to help keep dehydration at bay. Make sure you carry water with you wherever you go and drink plenty of it — don't just drink it when you're thirsty as this is a sign that your body is already dehydrated. Drinking water regularly is an efficient, effective and easy way to keep hydrated.

Stay out of the midday sun

The sun is strongest between 11 am and 3 pm, so avoid being in direct sunlight during this time by sitting in the shade under trees and canopies. Long periods in the sun can not only lead to sunburn, but also to heat exhaustion and heat stroke (see section below on 'heat exhaustion' for more information).

Heat exhaustion

Heat exhaustion is when the body can't cool down fast enough — if left untreated, it can easily develop into heat stroke, which can be life-threatening. Some of the symptoms of heat exhaustion include: nausea, headaches, dizziness and confusion — if you have any of these symptoms make sure you move immediately to the shade and drink plenty of cool water. If possible, sit in a cool bath or shower. If your symptoms persist, seek medical advice.

10) Identify and give an example of one language technique in the 'Stay hydrated' paragraph. Explain how it helps to convey meaning.

Technique: ....

Example from text: ....

....

Explanation of technique: ....

....

....

(3 marks)

11) You are going to give a talk about looking after your health before and during a holiday.

Using **Sources A and C**, write down **four** things from the texts that you will include in your talk. Make sure you only take information from the sources.

Four separate ideas to include in your talk:

1 ....

....

....

2 ....

....

....

3 ....

....

....

4 ....

....

....

(4 marks)

Reading Test 3

Give yourself **50 minutes** to do this test.

For multiple-choice questions, circle the letter you have chosen.
For longer answer questions, write your answers in the space provided.
You do not have to write in full sentences. You may use a dictionary.

Read **Source A** and answer questions 1-5.

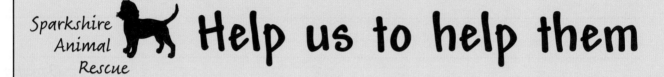

Sparkshire Animal Rescue — Help us to help them

Every year at Sparkshire Animal Rescue, we receive over 3000 calls relating to animals in need of our help. Our services range from advising people how to look after their pets to rescuing trapped and injured animals. We also take in abandoned and homeless pets and provide a rehoming service. But what can you do to make a difference? There are three ways you can help us to help them: by volunteering, donating or adopting.

Volunteering

Without our dedicated volunteers, there wouldn't be a Sparkshire Animal Rescue. We are always looking for enthusiastic and hard-working people who are willing to give up just a few hours a week to join our team. Duties range from filing paperwork, to walking our dogs or cleaning out cages.

Donations

Sparkshire Animal Rescue is a registered charity that works on a strictly voluntary basis. This means we desperately need donations in order to continue our work. A one-off donation of just £2 can feed two of our dogs for a day. Every donation, whether big or small, is put towards making our animals happier and helping them get a better quality of life. Isn't that money well spent?

Adoption

Each year, Sparkshire Animal Rescue takes in around 75 dogs and 100 cats that have been abandoned by their owners. If you think you could provide any of them with a loving home, we'd really like to hear from you. If you're interested in adopting one of our animals, you'll be asked to fill out a variety of forms. Once the forms have been processed and approved, a member of our team will contact you to arrange a home visit to make sure that the animals are re-homed with suitable owners. Please only apply if you can fully commit to the long-term care of a pet.

If you can help us to help them, in any way, please call us today on
06421 101010
We're really grateful for any contributions — and so are the animals!

1) Identify **two** persuasive language techniques used by the author.
Explain how these techniques persuade the reader to help the rescue centre and support your answer with quotes from the text.

....

....

....

....

....

....

(4 marks)

2) The leaflet informs you that:

a) You get paid for helping rescue animals

b) Only donations over £10 are useful

c) Sparkshire Animal Rescue is a charity

d) Volunteers only help with paperwork

(1 mark)

3) Using **Source A**, identify **two** ways someone could help Sparkshire Animal Rescue.

1 ....

2 ....

(2 marks)

4) Using **Source A**, identify **one** thing you would have to do before adopting an animal.

....

(1 mark)

5) Using **Source A**, identify **one** task that a volunteer could be responsible for.

....

(1 mark)

Read **Source B** and answer questions 6-9.

How to care for your rabbit

Rabbits are affectionate animals that can make great pets. Getting a new pet can be a really exciting time, but don't forget to follow these top tips to make sure you look after it properly.

Housing

It's important to make sure you provide a warm and waterproof house for your rabbit. The hutch you choose should be raised at least a foot from the ground so that damp doesn't rise up through the floor. You'll also need to make sure the roof is covered with a water-repellent material to keep your pet dry when it rains. Make sure you provide enough space for your rabbit to get enough exercise, too — a cramped bunny is not a happy bunny. Once you've arranged the hutch, fill it with a combination of hay and wood shavings.

Food

Like humans, rabbits need a well-balanced diet. It's best to feed your rabbit high-fibre pellets (which can be bought in most pet shops) as well as hay and a range of fresh vegetables. Fresh drinking water should be available to your pet at all times.

Vegetables for rabbits

✔ Cauliflower
✔ Celery
✔ Kale
✔ Broccoli
✔ Cucumber

Exercise

Rabbits are active animals that need lots of space to exercise — giving them a garden run would be ideal. You could also provide them with some cardboard tunnels (make sure they are big enough so your rabbit doesn't get stuck) to scamper through, so your rabbit can explore and exercise at the same time. It's also possible to buy leads and harnesses for small pets so you can take your rabbit for a walk — but make sure you don't take it near larger animals or roads, though.

Company

Rabbits are social animals — if they're kept alone, they will get lonely. Where possible, try to keep them in pairs. Rabbits like human interaction too, so make sure you give your pet lots of attention by stroking them. When handling, be careful and support your rabbit well.

For more information on how to care for your pets, visit:
www.pethelpcentre.co.uk

6) The article informs you that:

    a)   Rabbits like having company   c)   You can't keep rabbits outside

    b)   Rabbits should only be fed hay   d)   Rabbits are lazy animals

(1 mark)

7) The article suggests that:

    a)   Rabbits don't mind the rain   c)   Rabbits won't be happy in a small space

    b)   Rabbits can eat anything   d)   Rabbits don't like being stroked

(1 mark)

8) Your friend is worried that her rabbit isn't getting enough exercise. Using **Source B**, suggest how her pet could get more exercise.

....

....

....

....

(2 marks)

9) Identify **three** layout features of **Source B** that help convey the information.

Layout feature 1

....

....

Layout feature 2

....

....

Layout feature 3

....

....

(3 marks)

Read **Source C** and answer questions 10-12.

ZOOS: THE SHOCKING TRUTH

Zoos have always been popular visitor attractions, but we think it's time people knew the truth about these money-making organisations who only care about their profits and not their animals.

Would you like to be cramped in a small space with lots of other humans?

Many zoos think that simply sticking to the minimum space regulations is enough — it isn't. Experts have found that animals in zoos don't have the freedom to move around like they would in the wild. They get bored of being stuck in the same enclosure for years.

Would you like to do the same activities at the same time every day?

While many zoo animals are left with nothing to do, others are forced to perform shows and tricks. They're often forced into entertaining the crowds at regular intervals throughout the day. This would never happen in the wild.

Would you like to be moved from your home to a completely different location and environment?

Animals are often moved to places with a completely different climate to what they are used to. If they are used to living in a certain environment and are moved abruptly, they can find it extremely difficult to adapt and can become unhappy and ill. It also means leaving their family behind which can be incredibly traumatic.

Would you like to be forced to breed?

Studies show that zoos with cute baby animals attract 50% more customers — this encourages zoos to force their animals to breed, to increase their profits. Animals breed more successfully if they are comfortable (which is never the case in zoos) and being made to breed in captivity only leads to overpopulation, resulting in enclosures being even more cramped.

We're guessing you've answered 'no' to all of these questions — we did. If, like us, you think that zoos should be banned and animals should be left in their natural environments, please sign our petition today. Saving animals couldn't be easier.

10) Identify the **main** purpose of the leaflet.

....

....

(1 mark)

11) Say whether the following statements are presented in **Source C** as facts or as opinions.
Put a tick in the 'fact' column or the 'opinion' column.

	Fact	Opinion
Animals in zoos can become unhappy and ill.		
Animals in zoos don't have the freedom to move around like they would in the wild.		
Zoo animals are often forced to perform tricks.		
Studies show that zoos with cute baby animals attract 50% more customers.		
Zoos should be banned.		
Zoos only care about their profits.		

(3 marks)

12) You want your friend to understand the responsibilities humans have towards animals.
Using **Source B** and **Source C**, advise your friend on the responsibilities of humans towards animals.

....

....

....

....

....

....

....

....

....

(4 marks)

Reading Test 4

Give yourself **50 minutes** to do this test.

For multiple-choice questions, circle the letter you have chosen.
For longer answer questions, write your answers in the space provided.
You do not have to write in full sentences. You may use a dictionary.

Read **Source A** and answer questions 1-5.

DON'T DRINK-DRIVE

Every year, there are over 12,000 casualties as a direct result of drink-driving. Around 400 of these people die. Drink-driving problems have rocketed recently — we must take action and make our roads a safer place to drive.

Drinking alcohol affects your coordination, delays your reactions and can make your vision blurred. When you're driving, you rely on reaction, coordination and vision, and if these have been impaired by alcohol, the chance of an accident is significantly higher.

Many people feel sober after drinking 'lightly' and believe they are fit to drive, but the truth is they're often not. There's no set rule for how much you can drink before you're unsafe to drive — age, weight, gender, stress and metabolism can all affect how quickly you process alcohol. The legal limit in the UK for driving is 80 mg of alcohol per 100 ml of blood, and if you're found with more alcohol in your system, punishment is severe.

If you're caught drink-driving, you can expect to be banned from driving for a minimum of 12 months and receive a fine of up to £5,000. In some cases, you can be sent to prison.

If you do decide to go out and have a few drinks, make sure you have planned how to get home. You could nominate a driver (who won't drink any alcohol) to take you home, book a taxi and split the cost or take public transport. Whichever you choose, remember, drink-driving is <u>NOT</u> an option.

For more information on drink-driving, visit:
www.neverdrinkdrive.co.uk

1) The **main** purpose of the leaflet is to:

   a) Warn you about hazardous roads

   b) Persuade you to use public transport

   c) Tell you how dangerous drink-driving is

   d) Tell you not to drink on a night out

   (1 mark)

2) Identify **two** effects alcohol has on your driving.

   ....

   ....

   (2 marks)

3) Use **Source A** to give **one** example of something which affects our ability to process alcohol.

   ....

   (1 mark)

4) Is the tone of this leaflet personal or impersonal? ....

   How can you tell?

   ....

   ....

   (2 marks)

5) Use **Source A** to identify **one** way to make sure that you get home safely after a night out.

   ....

   (1 mark)

Read **Source B** and answer questions 6-9.

Operation Safe Driver

OPESD
Organisation for Post-Exam Safe Drivers

Just passing a driving test is no longer enough. Driving instructors are now insisting that motorists should take a course of post-exam driving lessons to improve their driving skills. The Organisation for Post-Exam Safe Drivers (OPESD) is offering courses, ranging from a day to two weeks, that can help to make drivers feel safer on the roads. OPESD courses aim to:

Teach drivers to be confident in a variety of different road conditions, such as driving in the snow, at night, on the motorway, on country lanes and in cities.

Encourage drivers to become more economical. Economical driving causes less wear and tear on the vehicle and can help lower fuel consumption, reducing the cost of motoring.

Make drivers more aware of hazards on the road and how they can avoid potential accidents.

OPESD are currently offering some great deals on driving courses:

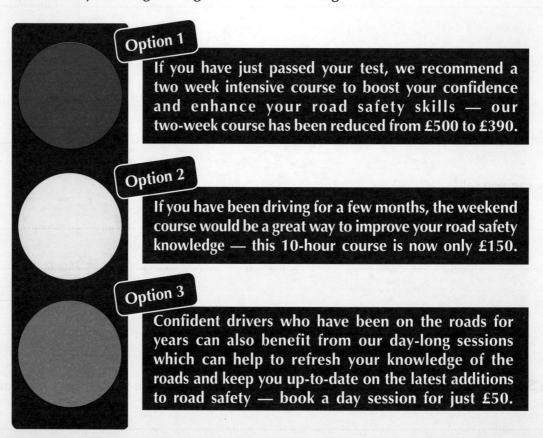

Option 1

If you have just passed your test, we recommend a two week intensive course to boost your confidence and enhance your road safety skills — our two-week course has been reduced from £500 to £390.

Option 2

If you have been driving for a few months, the weekend course would be a great way to improve your road safety knowledge — this 10-hour course is now only £150.

Option 3

Confident drivers who have been on the roads for years can also benefit from our day-long sessions which can help to refresh your knowledge of the roads and keep you up-to-date on the latest additions to road safety — book a day session for just £50.

Get in touch now on 021312 654321 to book your course.

6) What is the **main** purpose of the leaflet?

....

....

(1 mark)

7) Summarise the reasons why a new driver should take a course.

....

....

....

....

....

(3 marks)

8) Use **Source B** to identify **two** road conditions that an OPESD course could prepare you for.

....

....

(2 marks)

9) Your friend passed her test today and wants to learn how to drive in various road conditions. Which course would you recommend? Explain your choice.

Option ....

Explanation

....

....

(1 mark)

Read **Source C** and answer questions 10-12.

Safe Driving

Learning to drive is an exciting experience. Once you've passed your test, it's essential that you continue to drive carefully to keep yourself and other road users safe. Follow this advice to make sure you stay out of danger.

It's not just about how you drive — what you drive is important too. You'll need to make sure your vehicle is roadworthy. Do this by checking your oil and keeping it topped up to the correct level. You should check the level of your windscreen washer fluid and fill your washer bottle up before long journeys. You should also check the tread depth on your tyres is deep enough — the legal minimum tread depth in the UK is 1.6 mm across 75% of the tyre. If the tread on your tyres is getting close to this value, you'll need to get new ones to make

sure you stay safe. Similarly, if you notice anything different about your car, such as noises you've not heard before, get it checked at a garage.

You need to take into account your physical and mental state when driving anywhere. Tiredness reduces concentration, so if you're tired, you won't be safe to drive and you should avoid travelling until you feel more alert. Some prescription medicines can make you drowsy so check the packaging before driving.

Road safety is very important for keeping you and the people around you safe. Don't forget to keep up-to-date with the Highway Code. Speed restrictions and road signs are put in place for a reason, and you should always obey them — if you are stopped by a police officer, "I didn't see the sign!" isn't an acceptable excuse.

10) Use **Source C** to identify **two** vehicle checks you should make before going on a car journey.

....

....
(2 marks)

11) Which language feature is used in the sentence: "You'll need to make sure your vehicle is roadworthy"?

a) a slogan

c) the rule of three

b) direct address to the reader

d) a rhetorical question
(1 mark)

12) Look at **Sources B and C**. Which source uses presentational devices more effectively? Give **two** examples of presentational devices the source uses and say why they are effective.

Source .... uses presentational features more effectively.

Example 1: ....

....

Why it is effective...

....

....

....

Example 2: ....

....

Why it is effective...

....

....

....
(4 marks)

Answers to the Reading Questions

Please note, answers in bullet points are only suggestions. Any sensible alternative can be accepted.

Section One — How Ideas Are Presented

Page 5

Q1 To inform about the choir. Examples may vary. Some examples would be 'We are a local choir based at Stanhope Community Centre', 'The choir is a charitable organisation that was set up in 2008' or 'We perform at the Stanhope Festival every year'.

Q2 You could write any two of these:
- Stanhope Festival
- Town square
- County show

Q3 2008

Page 7

Q1 b — Women shouldn't work

Q2 d — Minna Williams is wrong

Q3 Truman Williams

Q4 To argue that Minna Williams is wrong.
Examples may vary. Some examples would be 'But what she said yesterday was completely unacceptable' or 'She is a disgrace and doesn't deserve to call herself a woman'.

Page 9

Q1 You could write any two of these:
- To inform the reader about the increase in cycling.
Examples may vary. For example, 'there has been a noticeable rise in the number of people out and about on their bikes'.
- To inform people about the benefits of cycling.
Examples may vary. For example, 'it's a great way to get around'.
- To persuade the reader to go cycling.
Examples may vary. For example, 'So why not have a go yourself?'

Q2 You could write any two of these:
- To describe the Eiffel Tower.
Examples may vary. For example, 'The Eiffel Tower is an architectural beauty'.
- To advise people about visiting the Eiffel Tower.

Examples may vary. For example, 'you need to get there early'.
- To inform the reader about the Eiffel Tower.
Examples may vary. For example, 'Tickets cost between €5 and €15'.

Page 11

Q1 a) fact
b) opinion
c) opinion
d) fact

Q2 Fact
Opinion
Fact
Opinion
Fact
Fact

Q3 You could write any one of these:
- 16% of bar and pub owners have noticed a significant drop in business.
- The number of people suffering heart attacks has fallen by more than 2%.

Page 13

Q1 You could write any one of these:
- The writer has exaggerated how popular Mr Warhurst is.
- The writer hasn't supported what he says with any evidence.
Examples may vary. Some examples would be 'Mr Warhurst is the best MP Gawesbury has ever seen' or 'all the locals' support'.

Q2 You could write any two of these:
- The writer has used strong language.
Examples may vary. For example 'outraged', 'horrendous', 'hideous'.
- The writer has used humour.
Examples may vary. For example, 'it made my hair greasier than a plate of chips.'
- The writer has exaggerated how bad the shampoo is.
Examples may vary. For example 'the product itself smelt horrendous'.

Page 15

Q1 Advert

Q2 You could write any one of these:
- Bullet points
- Coloured text
- Picture
- Interesting font

- The name 'Shear Hairdressing'
- The 'Cuts for £10' graphic

Q3 Website

Q4 You could write any of these:
- Address bar
- Search box
- Links to other pages

Q5 Article

Q6 You could write any of these:
- Headline
- Columns
- Subheadings

Q7 Email

Q8 You could write any of these:
- 'To' box
- 'Subject' box
- Send or envelope button
- Box for text

Page 17

Q1 a) Headline / title
b) You could write any one of these:
- Grabs the reader's attention.
- Tells the reader what the text is about.

Q2 a) Subheading
b) You could write any one of these:
- Breaks up the text.
- Tells the reader what the section is about.

Q3 a) Columns
b) Makes the text easier to read.

Q4 a) Bullet points
b) You could write any one of these:
- Separates the information.
- Makes the text easier to read.

Page 19

Q1 You could write any one of these:
- Makes the important information stand out.
- Makes the reader look at it first.

Q2 You could write any one of these:
- Helps the reader know what the text is about before they have read it.
- It makes the text more interesting to read.
- Grabs the reader's attention.

Q3 c — To make it stand out

Q4 You could write any two of these:
- Headline / Title
- Bold font
- Coloured text
- Graphic/logo
- Bullet points

Q5 Answers may vary. For example:
- Bullet points — break up the information.
- Bold font — grabs the reader's attention

Page 21

Q1 a — Rule of three
   c — Rhetorical question

Q2 Rule of three examples: 'impressive building, fascinating history and breathtaking surroundings' or 'our beautiful castle, its beautiful grounds and the beautiful landscape.' Rhetorical question examples: 'Is there a better way to spend a day than exploring Yewbarrow Castle?' or 'who doesn't like getting lost now and again?'

Q3 c — Alliteration

Q4 Direct address to the reader and the rule of three.

Page 23

Q1 a) Idiom
   b) Metaphor
   c) Simile

Q2 a — A metaphor

Q3 It helps the reader to imagine the impact the novel had on the writer.

Q4 To reveal something without meaning to.

Q5 You could write any one of these:
- 'I feel like a child about to open their birthday presents.'
- 'Waiting for a book to be released is like getting ready to set off on an adventure'.

Page 25

Q1 a) Personal
   b) You could write any one of these:
- It uses words like 'we' and 'you'.
- It says what the writer thinks.

Q2 b — The wedding is going to be casual

Q3 a) Informal

b) You could write any one of these:
- It sounds chatty.
- It doesn't sound serious.
- It uses shortened words.
- It uses slang.

Q4 c — It matches the style of the wedding

Section Two — Finding Information From Texts

Page 27

Q1 Source A
Q2 Source C
Q3 Source B

Page 29

Q1 b — To tell the reader about a horse's diet

Q2 You could write any one of these:
- Grass
- Herbs
- Weeds

Q3 d — Oats

Q4 So that the horse can drink from it.

Q5 Hay

Page 31

Q1 April 28th

Q2 48 Morley Road, Smithsgate Retail Park

Q3 d — McIntyre Classic Dresser

Q4 c — £750.00

Q5 You could write any one of these:
- Standford Office Desk
- McIntyre Classic Dresser

Page 33

Q1 b — Hythes Housing

Q2 On the site of the derelict playground near to St Paul's churchyard.

Q3 You could write any one of these:
- By visiting the forum
- www.hendleyissues.forum.

Q4 A new play area

Q5 You could write any two of these:
- She says that they "can reach a solution that is acceptable to everyone".
- It is an "exciting new scheme".
- "everyone will benefit, including local people".

Page 35

Q1 Source B

Q2 You could write any four of these:
- Go for a power walk at lunchtime
- Go for a jog before dinner
- Do a workout DVD at home

- Join a sports club
- Walk to school

Reading Test Practice

Page 38

Q1 b — You might get injured swimming

Q2 To persuade you to visit Mark Pitt for a physio session.

Q3 You could write any two of these (reasons may vary):
- Large headline / title — it grabs the reader's attention / tells the reader what the text is about.
- Bullet points — they help to separate the information / make the text easier to read / make the text clear.
- Bold subheadings / coloured subheadings — they separate the information / make key ideas stand out / tell the reader what the section is about.
- Photo — it backs up the ideas in the text / grabs the reader's attention / makes the text more interesting.

Reading Test Practice

You should be aiming to get around fifteen marks and above in these reading exercises to pass.

Practice Reading Test 1

Source A (Pages 40-41)

Q1 c — Inform you how to eat more healthily

Q2 You could write any of these:
- Most adults don't eat their five a day.
- There are high levels of obesity.
- People are having to think more carefully about how what they eat affects their health.

Q3 You could write any three of these:
- Add chopped fruit or berries to porridge.
- Drink a glass of fruit juice with your breakfast.
- Eat carrot sticks as a healthy snack.
- Finely chop peppers or carrots and add them to sauces.

Q4 You could write any two of these:
- You sleep better.
- You have clearer skin.
- You have more energy.
- You can concentrate more.
- It might help you lose weight.

Answers to the Reading Questions

Source B (Pages 42-43)

Q5 To tell you about the dangers of crash diets. Supporting text may vary. For example, the title says diets pose a "risk" to health.

Q6 You could write any one of these:
- 'Consuming such a low number of calories a day drastically reduces how much energy we have'
- 'reduces concentration levels'.
- 'shakiness and even memory loss'.
- 'it can cause all sorts of health problems. Malnutrition is one of them'.
- 'a single energy drink cannot possibly provide all the essential vitamins and minerals that a healthy balanced diet would provide.'

Q7 c — a rhetorical question

Q8 You could write any two of these:
- Boxes for different crash diets separate the information and make it easy to read.
- Photos make the text interesting to read / grab the reader's attention.
- Coloured boxes / bright colours catch the reader's eye.
- Headline tells you what the article is about.
- Columns make the text easier to read.
- Bold text highlights the key words.

Q9 You could write any two of these:
- Reduce energy levels
- Reduce level of concentration
- Shakiness
- Memory loss
- Malnutrition

Source C (Pages 44-45)

Q10 b — Persuade you to join one of the gyms

Q11 Gym 2
Reason: He has the goal of completing a triathlon and Target Central aims to help people reach their individual "fitness target".

Q12 Answers may vary. Example:
- Gym 1
- Reason 1: Because I want to lose weight.
- Reason 2: Because I want to use the sauna.
- Reason 3: Because I want to be given a personal diet and exercise plan.

Practice Reading Test 2

Source A (Pages 46-47)

Q1 You could write any of these:
- EHIC cards make medical treatment abroad cheaper.
- You can get them for free by filling out a simple form.

Q2 c — You should prepare for your trip well

Q3 You could write any of these:
- It is a document essential for overseas travel.
- To remind the reader to take a passport.

Q4 You could write any of these (supporting text may vary):
- Purpose: to inform you about what you need to go travelling. Supporting text: 'A passport is vital for travelling outside the UK.'
- Purpose: to advise you how to prepare for travelling. Supporting text: 'Find out if there is a risk of malaria where you are going and consult your GP.'

Source B (Pages 48-49)

Q5 b — Long-haul flights are harming the planet

Q6 c — Rose by 100m tonnes during 2006-2007

Q7 They will increase

Q8 You could write any of these:
- It is biased/only gives one side of the argument. Examples may vary. For example, 'But this convenient way of travelling is costing the planet dearly.'
- Using opinions. Examples may vary. For example, 'we must learn to live with the guilt of damaging the environment'.
- Using facts. Examples may vary. For example, 'Every year, around 700 million tonnes of carbon emissions are released into the atmosphere'.
- Using strong language. Examples may vary. For example, 'this method of travel is severely harming the environment'.

Q9 You could write any of these:
- Recycling.
- Walking or cycling instead of driving.
- Using solar panels to power their homes.

Source C (Pages 50-51)

Q10 You could write any of these:
- Technique: Idiom
- Example: 'This is important to help keep dehydration at bay.'
- Explanation: It is more interesting than just writing 'This is important to stop dehydration'.
- Technique: Direct address to the reader.
- Example: 'Make sure you drink plenty of fluids, ideally water, when it's hot.'
- Explanation: It makes the advice feel personal to the reader.
- Technique: Rule of three
- Example: 'Drinking water regularly is an efficient, effective and easy way to keep hydrated.'
- Explanation: It emphasises to the reader how important drinking water is.

Q11 You could write any four of these:
- Find out what vaccines you need, and when you need them, by going to see your GP.
- Check to see if you need antimalaria drugs.
- Get travel insurance to cover any medical treatment.
- Get an EHIC for cheaper medical treatment in Europe.
- Use sun cream to protect you from the sun and apply it regularly.
- Drink plenty of water if you're travelling in a hot country so you don't suffer from dehydration.
- Stay out of the midday sun to avoid heat exhaustion and heat stroke.
- If you feel dizzy or ill after being in the sun, seek medical advice as you could have heat exhaustion.

Practice Reading Test 3

Source A (Pages 52-53)

Q1 Slogan: Stays in the readers mind. Supporting text: 'Help us to help them.'
Rhetorical question: Persuades reader that they should help. Supporting text: 'But what can you do to make a difference?' or 'Isn't that money well spent?'

Answers to the Reading Questions

Direct address to the reader:
Feels personal, making the
reader more likely to be
persuaded.
Supporting text: 'There are
three ways you can help us to
help them'.

Q2 c — Sparkshire Animal Rescue
is a charity

Q3 You could write any two of
these:
  • Become a volunteer at the
  centre.
  • Make a donation to the
  centre.
  • Adopt one of the centre's
  animals.

Q4 You could write any one of
these:
  • Fill out a variety of forms.
  • Arrange a home visit.

Q5 You could write any one of
these:
  • Filing paperwork.
  • Walking the centre's dogs.
  • Cleaning out cages.

Source B (Pages 54-55)

Q6 a — Rabbits like having
company

Q7 c — Rabbits won't be happy in a
small space

Q8 You could write any of these:
  • Give the rabbit a garden run.
  • Give them some cardboard
  tunnels to scamper through.
  • Buy a harness and take it for a
  walk.

Q9 You could write any three of
these:
  • Bold/coloured titles make it
  easy to find information.
  • Bullet points for vegetables
  separate the information and
  make it easy to read.
  • Photos make the text
  interesting to read.
  • Text boxes separate the
  information and make it easier
  to read.
  • Headline tells you what the
  text is about.

Source C (Pages 56-57)

Q10 To persuade people to sign the
petition.

Q11 Fact
Fact
Fact
Fact

Opinion
Opinion
For 0-1 correct — 0 marks.
For 2-3 correct — 1 mark.
For 4-5 correct — 2 marks.
For 6 correct — 3 marks.

Q12 You could write any of these:
  • Animals shouldn't be kept in
  enclosed spaces (B+C)
  • Animals need exercise and
  things to do (B+C)
  • Pets need comfortable and safe
  housing (B)
  • Pets need lots of attention (B)
  • Pets need a well-balanced diet (B)
  • Animals in zoos shouldn't be
  forced to entertain people and
  perform tricks (C)
  • Animals shouldn't be separated
  from their families and moved
  somewhere they're going to find it
  difficult to adapt to (C)
  • Zoo animals shouldn't be forced
  to breed (C)

Practice Reading Test 4

Source A (Pages 58-59)

Q1 c — Tell you how dangerous
drink-driving is

Q2 You could write any two of these:
  • Affects coordination.
  • Slows your reactions.
  • Affects your vision.

Q3 You could write any one of these:
  • Age.
  • Weight.
  • Gender.
  • Stress.
  • Metabolism.

Q4 personal
You could write any one of these:
  • It uses words like 'you' and 'we'.
  • It sounds like it's talking to the
  reader.

Q5 You could write any of these:
  • Nominate a driver who is not
  going to drink alcohol.
  • Book a taxi.
  • Use public transport.

Source B (Pages 60-61)

Q6 To persuade you to take a driving
course with OPESD.

Q7 You could write any of these:
  • To improve their confidence in
  different road conditions.
  • To improve their road safety
  skills and avoid accidents.

  • To learn to drive more
  economically.

Q8 You could write any two of these:
  • snow
  • at night
  • motorways
  • country lanes
  • cities

Q9 Option 1
  • Explanation: She has just passed
  her test and option 1 is for drivers
  who have just passed their test.

Source C (Pages 62-63)

Q10 You could write any two of these:
  • Make sure your oil is topped up
  to the correct level.
  • Fill up your windscreen washer
  bottle.
  • Check the tread depth on your
  tyres.
  • Make sure your car isn't doing
  anything unusual before setting off.

Q11 b — direct address to the reader.

Q12 You could choose either source.

Source B
You could write any two of these:
  • Headline / title. Reasons may
  vary. It's eye-catching / it tells the
  reader what the text is about.
  • Logo / graphic. Reasons may
  vary. It helps the reader know
  what the text is about / it makes
  the text more interesting to read /
  it's eye-catching.
  • Bullet points. Reasons may
  vary. They separate each piece of
  information / they make the text
  easier to read.
  • Large or bold text. Reasons may
  vary. It makes the most important
  information stand out (for example
  the telephone number at the
  bottom).
  • Coloured background. Reasons
  may vary. It makes the text eye-
  catching / more interesting to read.

Source C
You could write any two of these:
  • Paragraphs. Reasons may vary.
  They split up the text / make the
  information easier to read.
  • Bold text. It catches the
  reader's attention.
  • Headline / title. It tells the
  reader what the text is about.
  • Columns. Reasons may vary.
  It breaks up the text / makes the
  text easier to read.

Answers to the Reading Questions

Knowing Your Audience and Purpose

Audience and purpose are important

1) An **audience** is the **person or people** who read a text.

2) You need to know who your **audience** is so you can decide whether your writing should be **formal** or **informal**.

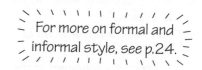
For more on formal and informal style, see p.24.

3) The **purpose** of a text is the **reason** it is written. For example, to **inform** or **persuade**.

Find out who you are writing for and why

In the writing test, use the question to tell you **who** the text is for and **why** you are writing it.

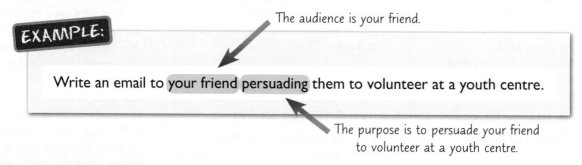

EXAMPLE:

The audience is your friend.

Write an email to your friend persuading them to volunteer at a youth centre.

The purpose is to persuade your friend to volunteer at a youth centre.

Use the right writing style

Make sure your **writing style** is **suitable** for the **audience** and the **purpose**.

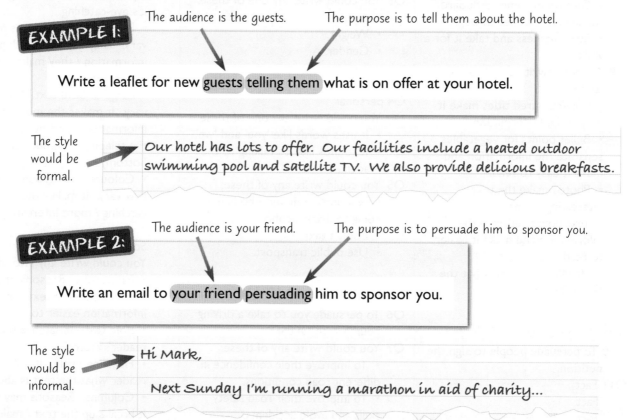

EXAMPLE 1:

The audience is the guests.

The purpose is to tell them about the hotel.

Write a leaflet for new guests telling them what is on offer at your hotel.

The style would be formal.

Our hotel has lots to offer. Our facilities include a heated outdoor swimming pool and satellite TV. We also provide delicious breakfasts.

EXAMPLE 2:

The audience is your friend.

The purpose is to persuade him to sponsor you.

Write an email to your friend persuading him to sponsor you.

The style would be informal.

Hi Mark,

Next Sunday I'm running a marathon in aid of charity...

Practice Questions

1) Write down the audience and purpose for each of these writing tasks.

   a) Write a leaflet for tourists explaining what there is to do in your town.

   Audience ....

   Purpose ....

   b) Write an email to your council complaining about the lack of recycling facilities in your area.

   Audience ....

   Purpose ....

   c) Write a letter applying for volunteer work in a charity shop.

   Audience ....

   Purpose ....

   d) Write a letter to your boss persuading them to give you flexible working hours.

   Audience ....

   Purpose ....

   e) Write an article for a newspaper advising people how to save money.

   Audience ....

   Purpose ....

2) Formal writing is for people you don't know or people in charge.
   Informal writing is for people you know well.

   What type of writing style would you use for these writing tasks? Circle 'Formal' or 'Informal'.

   a) A letter to a neighbour asking them to feed your cat   Formal / Informal

   b) An email to a supermarket complaining about mouldy food   Formal / Informal

   c) A film review for your local newspaper   Formal / Informal

   d) A leaflet about burglaries to be delivered along your street   Formal / Informal

   e) An email to your sister inviting her to your party   Formal / Informal

Planning Your Answer

Make a plan before you start writing

1) Planning your answer will help you put your ideas **in order**.

2) A plan **doesn't** need to be in full sentences. Just write down your **key** ideas to **save time**.

3) Make sure you **only** write down points that **answer the question**.

4) In the test, you can write a plan in your **answer booklet**.

Use notes to write your plan

1) Work out the **audience** and **purpose** and whether you should be **formal** or **informal**.

2) Write down the **points** you want to include.

3) **Organise** your points so that the **most important** ideas come **first**.

4) If you're given **bullet points** in the test, you could include them in your plan.

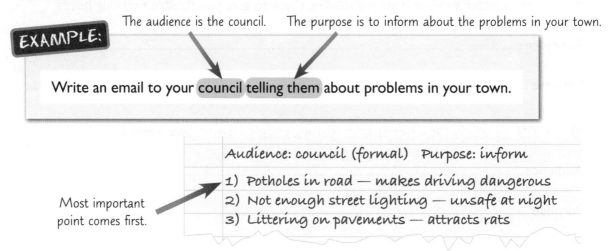

EXAMPLE:

The audience is the council.   The purpose is to inform about the problems in your town.

Write an email to your council telling them about problems in your town.

Audience: council (formal)   Purpose: inform

Most important point comes first.

1) Potholes in road — makes driving dangerous
2) Not enough street lighting — unsafe at night
3) Littering on pavements — attracts rats

How to plan letters and emails

1) Work out who the audience is to decide if your writing should be **formal** or **informal**.

2) This will help you decide which **greeting** and **ending** to use (see p.78).

3) Your first paragraph should tell the reader **why** you are writing to them.

4) The main body of the letter or email should **develop** your ideas and give more **detail**.

5) The last paragraph should tell the reader what **action** you want them to take.

Planning Your Answer

How to plan an article

Work out your **purpose** and **audience**. Think about **where** the article will be printed.

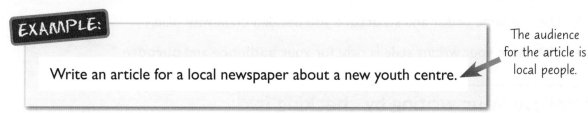

EXAMPLE:

Write an article for a local newspaper about a new youth centre.

The audience for the article is local people.

Start with the main facts. What it is, where it is and when it opened.

Audience: newspaper readers (formal)   Purpose: to inform
1) Youth centre / Herman Road / opened last week
2) Council funded / offers sports and evening classes

Then go into detail about the subject.

How to plan a report

The purpose of a report is to **give information**. It needs to be **clear** and **accurate**.

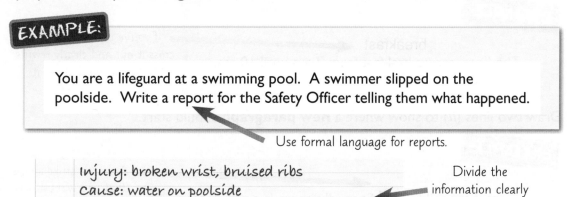

EXAMPLE:

You are a lifeguard at a swimming pool. A swimmer slipped on the poolside. Write a report for the Safety Officer telling them what happened.

Use formal language for reports.

Injury: broken wrist, bruised ribs
Cause: water on poolside
Solution: safety signs, more cleaning

Divide the information clearly into sections.

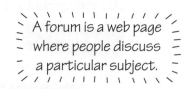

A forum is a web page where people discuss a particular subject.

How to plan a forum response or a review

1) The purpose of these text types is to **give** your **opinion** and **argue** a point of view.

2) Your **first point** should clearly explain your main argument.

3) You'll get better marks if your **argument** is **balanced**.

4) So remember to include a point or two from the **other side** of the argument.

5) The rest of your points should **back up** your **argument**. Use P.E.E.

6) Use **persuasive language** to convince people of your point of view.

See p.74 for more on P.E.E.

Writing and Checking Your Answer

Use your plan to write your answer

1) Put the ideas in your plan into **full sentences**.

2) Use the same **order** and **structure** you decided on in your plan.

3) Make sure your writing style is right for your **audience** and **purpose**.

Improve your writing by checking it

1) Read over your answer carefully and **make improvements**.

2) Take out anything you **don't need**.

3) Don't **repeat** yourself. Make each point **once**.

4) Check that your **spelling**, **punctuation** and **grammar** are correct.

> Make sure you leave enough time to read through your answer.

Make sure your corrections are neat

1) **Cross out** any **mistakes** neatly and **write** any corrections **above** them.

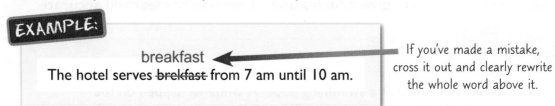

EXAMPLE:

breakfast

The hotel serves ~~brekfast~~ from 7 am until 10 am.

If you've made a mistake, cross it out and clearly rewrite the whole word above it.

2) Draw two lines (*//*) to show where a **new paragraph** should start.

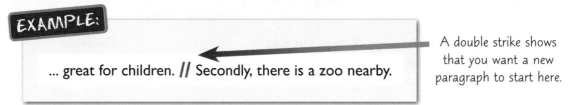

EXAMPLE:

... great for children. **//** Secondly, there is a zoo nearby.

A double strike shows that you want a new paragraph to start here.

3) Use the symbol ∧ below the line to **add** in a **missing word**.

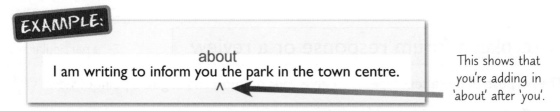

EXAMPLE:

about

I am writing to inform you the park in the town centre.

∧

This shows that you're adding in 'about' after 'you'.

4) Use a **star** if you need to **add** in **more** than one word.

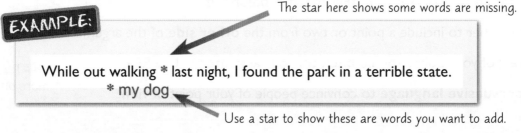

The star here shows some words are missing.

EXAMPLE:

While out walking * last night, I found the park in a terrible state.

* my dog

Use a star to show these are words you want to add.

Practice Question

1) Read the following writing task and the example plan for an answer.

> You are planning a day out at a theme park.
> Write an email to your friends encouraging them to come with you.

> Audience: your friends (informal)   Purpose: persuade / inform
>
> Details
> * What: Day out at a theme park
> * When: May 22nd — leave at 8 am, arrive by 10 am
> * Where: Talltown Towers — directions / take train to Uxley
>
> Anything else
> * Bring waterproofs — you will get wet on some rides
> * Other friends welcome
> * Half-price tickets if you book online

Remember to start a new paragraph every time you talk about a new bullet point.

Turn this plan into a full answer. Make improvements and add details as you write.

....

....

....

....

....

....

....

....

....

....

....

Using Paragraphs

Paragraphs make your writing easier to read

1) A paragraph is a **group of sentences**.

2) These sentences talk about the **same thing** or **follow on** from each other.

Divide your plan into paragraphs

1) You could give each **point** in your plan its own **paragraph**.

2) Start with an **introduction** paragraph. It should **summarise** what your answer is about.

3) Make your last paragraph a **conclusion**. It should **sum up** your main point.

Use paragraphs to show when something changes

1) Start a new paragraph when you talk about a different **topic**, **person**, **place** or **time**.

2) To show a new paragraph, start a new line and leave a **space** at the beginning.

Leave a space to show it's a new paragraph.

Different person.

Different place.

Surveys suggest that Ulrow shoppers are leaving Christmas shopping later each year. Start a new paragraph on a new line.
Bill Todd, a local shop-owner, said that last year the busiest day in the festive period was Christmas Eve.
In Barston, the trend is very different. Similar surveys show that the week running up to Christmas is their quietest.

3) You will **lose marks** if your writing isn't in paragraphs.

Your paragraphs should usually be longer than one sentence.

Use P.E.E. to develop your points

P.E.E. stands for **Point, Example, Explanation**. It helps to **structure** your paragraphs.

Make your <u>point</u> first.   Give an <u>example</u> of your point.

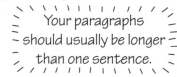

Using an officially registered gas engineer is important. Each year, hundreds of people are hospitalised because of unsafe gas work. Nearly all of these incidents were caused by unregistered gas engineers not doing a proper job.

<u>Explain</u> how the example backs up your point.

Practice Question

1) Read this piece of writing about coffee shops.
   Rewrite it underneath with new paragraphs in the correct places.

New coffee shops are opening up every day in the UK. It is thought that the number of coffee shops will double in just a few years. Some people believe that the British interest in coffee began in 1978, when the first coffee shops opened in London. When it became clear that these shops were making a lot of money, more and more began appearing all over the country. Last year, over two billion pounds worth of coffee was sold. The biggest coffee chains sell just under half a million cups of coffee every day. However, not everyone likes coffee. Surveys suggest that 16% of the population have never visited a coffee shop.

Writing Emails

You need to be able to write different text types

1) In the writing exam, you'll be asked to write **two** different **text types**.

2) Text types are just different ways of **presenting information**, like an **email** or a **report**.

3) You will get **marks** for how you **set out** your text.

4) For example, you'll get marks for setting out a **letter** correctly.

5) But don't worry about writing in **columns** or adding **pictures**.

6) Remember it's a writing test, so focus on the **content** and the **structure** of your answer.

Make sure the style of your email is right for the audience

1) When you email a **company** or **someone important**, use **formal** language.

2) You should also use **formal** language if you're emailing someone you **don't know**.

3) Emails to **family** and **friends** can be more **informal**.

Lay out emails correctly

Make sure you include all the **right information**.

In the exam you'll usually be given an email template to write your answer in.

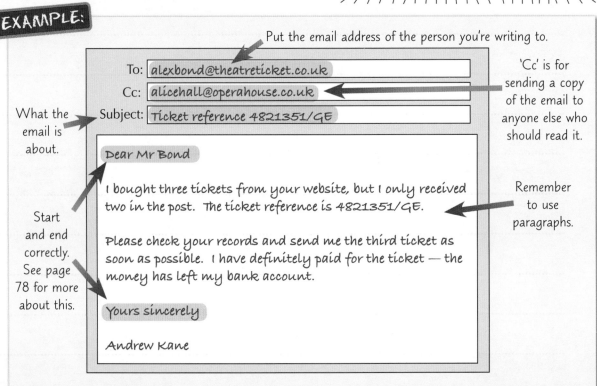

EXAMPLE:

Put the email address of the person you're writing to.

To: alexbond@theatreticket.co.uk

Cc: alicehall@operahouse.co.uk

'Cc' is for sending a copy of the email to anyone else who should read it.

What the email is about. → Subject: Ticket reference 4821351/GE

Dear Mr Bond

I bought three tickets from your website, but I only received two in the post. The ticket reference is 4821351/GE.

Please check your records and send me the third ticket as soon as possible. I have definitely paid for the ticket — the money has left my bank account.

Start and end correctly. See page 78 for more about this.

Remember to use paragraphs.

Yours sincerely

Andrew Kane

Practice Question

1) Read this email from a co-worker about the office Christmas party.

	From:	harry.coates@officemail.co.uk
✉	To:	you@officemail.co.uk
Send	Subject:	Christmas party

Hello

I'm organising the Christmas party this year, and I'm looking for some help to put it together. We're holding the party at the Armadillo Hotel on Wednesday 21st December. It would be great if a few of you could help me put up some decorations, book the DJ and organise the food.

Let me know if you'd like to help out. Any ideas or suggestions for the party would be great.

Cheers
Harry

Write a short reply which:

- tells Harry that you would like to help organise the party

- says how you would like to help out

- gives any suggestions you have for the party

Use the space below to plan your answer. Write your answer on a separate piece of paper. Make sure your spelling, punctuation and grammar are correct.

Writing Letters

Formal letters are for people you don't know

1) Start with a **formal greeting**. For example, 'Dear Sir/Madam' or 'Dear Mr Jones'.

2) **End** with 'Yours sincerely' if you know their name, or 'Yours faithfully' if you don't.

3) Avoid **slang**, **exclamation marks**, **abbreviations** and **text language**.

Informal letters are for people you know well

1) Start with the **name** of who you're sending it to.

2) **End** with something like '**Best wishes**' or '**See you soon**'.

3) You can be more **chatty**, but make sure your spelling and grammar are correct.

Follow the rules for writing letters

There are some things that all **letters** need.

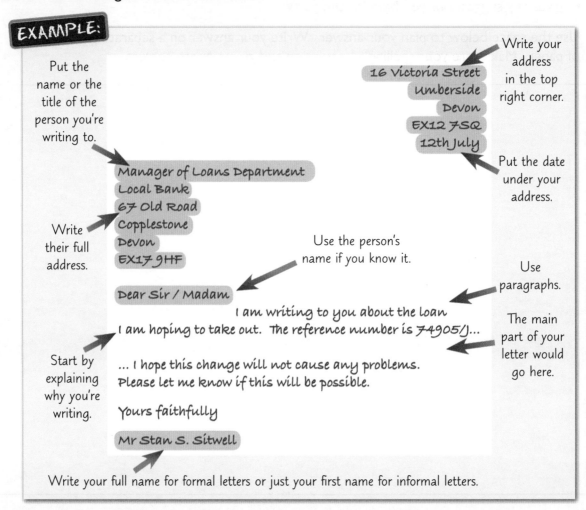

EXAMPLE:

Put the name or the title of the person you're writing to.

Write their full address.

Start by explaining why you're writing.

16 Victoria Street
Umberside
Devon
EX12 7SQ
12th July

Manager of Loans Department
Local Bank
67 Old Road
Copplestone
Devon
EX17 9HF

Dear Sir / Madam

I am writing to you about the loan I am hoping to take out. The reference number is 74905/J...

... I hope this change will not cause any problems. Please let me know if this will be possible.

Yours faithfully

Mr Stan S. Sitwell

Write your address in the top right corner.

Put the date under your address.

Use the person's name if you know it.

Use paragraphs.

The main part of your letter would go here.

Write your full name for formal letters or just your first name for informal letters.

Practice Question

1) You see the advert below.

> Mitterdon Community Centre is a local centre where young people can learn new skills, play sports and engage in team-bonding exercises in a safe environment. We are looking for someone to volunteer to run a sports or craft programme. Please contact Mrs Susan Holt to apply. The address is: Mitterdon Community Centre, 19 Church Street, Stockport, SK8 7DN. Remember to include any relevant experience you might have and a brief explanation of why you would be the right person for the role.

Write a letter to volunteer for the organisation described above. Think about:

- the layout of the letter

- the content of the letter

- the tone of the letter and who you are writing for

Use the space below to plan your answer. Write your answer on a separate piece of paper. Make sure your spelling, punctuation and grammar are correct.

Writing Articles

Articles appear in newspapers or magazines

1) Articles are usually **formal** texts which **inform** the reader about something.

2) When you're writing an article, you might want to **persuade** the reader to **agree** with your **point of view**.

3) Use **facts** and **figures** to **provide information** and to **support** your **opinion**.

Think about the structure of your article

An answer to an **article question** might look like this.

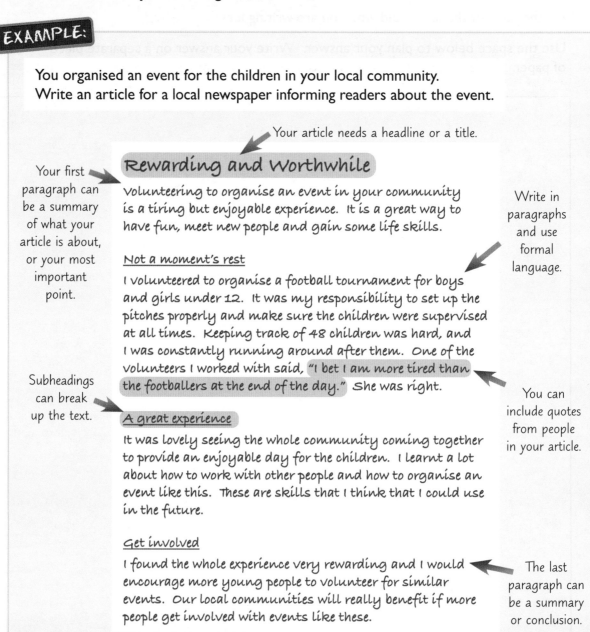

EXAMPLE:

You organised an event for the children in your local community.
Write an article for a local newspaper informing readers about the event.

Your article needs a headline or a title.

Rewarding and Worthwhile

Your first paragraph can be a summary of what your article is about, or your most important point.

Volunteering to organise an event in your community is a tiring but enjoyable experience. It is a great way to have fun, meet new people and gain some life skills.

Write in paragraphs and use formal language.

Not a moment's rest

I volunteered to organise a football tournament for boys and girls under 12. It was my responsibility to set up the pitches properly and make sure the children were supervised at all times. Keeping track of 48 children was hard, and I was constantly running around after them. One of the volunteers I worked with said, "I bet I am more tired than the footballers at the end of the day." She was right.

Subheadings can break up the text.

A great experience

You can include quotes from people in your article.

It was lovely seeing the whole community coming together to provide an enjoyable day for the children. I learnt a lot about how to work with other people and how to organise an event like this. These are skills that I think that I could use in the future.

Get involved

I found the whole experience very rewarding and I would encourage more young people to volunteer for similar events. Our local communities will really benefit if more people get involved with events like these.

The last paragraph can be a summary or conclusion.

Practice Question

1) You went to the event below.

> **Charity Dinner for the Jane Bauer Foundation**
> On Saturday 21st September the Jane Bauer Foundation held a charity dinner in order to raise money for the local hospital. The dinner included an auction, a speech by the head of the Jane Bauer Foundation (Mr James Johnson) and a raffle with a selection of great prizes. The event raised more than its target of £2,500.

Write a newspaper article about the event. Think about:

• the layout of your article

• the content of the article

• the tone of the article and who you are writing for

Use the space below to plan your answer. Write your answer on a separate piece of paper. Make sure your spelling, punctuation and grammar are correct.

Writing Reports

Reports provide information

1) Reports give the reader **information** and **recommendations** about something.

2) They need to be **formal** and **informative**.

Reports summarise an issue

1) Write an **introduction** for your report to **explain** the issue you're writing about.

2) The main part of your report will **summarise** the **important points** about the issue.

3) In your **conclusion** you'll give your **advice** or **opinion** about the issue.

Reports should be balanced

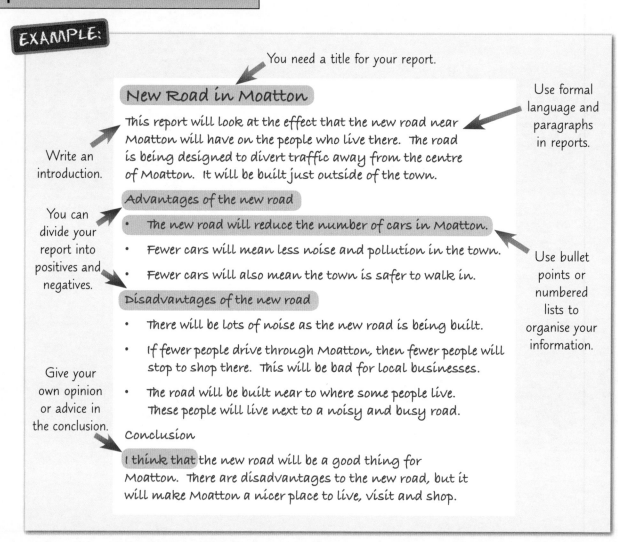

EXAMPLE:

You need a title for your report.

New Road in Moatton

Write an introduction.

This report will look at the effect that the new road near Moatton will have on the people who live there. The road is being designed to divert traffic away from the centre of Moatton. It will be built just outside of the town.

Use formal language and paragraphs in reports.

Advantages of the new road

You can divide your report into positives and negatives.

- The new road will reduce the number of cars in Moatton.
- Fewer cars will mean less noise and pollution in the town.
- Fewer cars will also mean the town is safer to walk in.

Use bullet points or numbered lists to organise your information.

Disadvantages of the new road

- There will be lots of noise as the new road is being built.
- If fewer people drive through Moatton, then fewer people will stop to shop there. This will be bad for local businesses.
- The road will be built near to where some people live. These people will live next to a noisy and busy road.

Give your own opinion or advice in the conclusion.

Conclusion

I think that the new road will be a good thing for Moatton. There are disadvantages to the new road, but it will make Moatton a nicer place to live, visit and shop.

Practice Question

1) Read the article below.

> **Burnham Community Theatre to Close**
>
> It was announced today that Burnham Community Theatre will close to make way for a new car park in the town centre. The Community Theatre, which provided Saturday drama classes for children, has been an important part of Burnham for 15 years. At one point, the Theatre staged a new play every fortnight, and its Christmas pantomime sold out every year. Burnham's theatre goers will now have to travel up to 50 miles to see a play. Some residents are in favour of the new car park because it will create 460 parking spaces and will help to reduce parking problems in Burnham. Businesses and shops in the town centre believe that the new car park will help attract shoppers and boost their sales.

Write a report about how the council's plans might affect Burnham. Think about:

• the positives of the new car park

• the negatives of the Community Theatre closing

Use the space below to plan your answer. Write your answer on a separate piece of paper. Make sure your spelling, punctuation and grammar are correct.

Writing Leaflets

Leaflets can have different purposes

1) Leaflets often provide **information** about something. For example, buying a house.

2) Leaflets can also **persuade** a reader to do something. For example, donate blood.

Know who your audience is

1) You need to make sure the **language** and **style** used in the leaflet **suits** its **audience**.

2) You might use **formal** and **serious language** for a leaflet about fire hazards at home.

3) You might use **chatty** language for a leaflet **persuading** readers to visit a museum.

The information in a leaflet needs to be laid out clearly

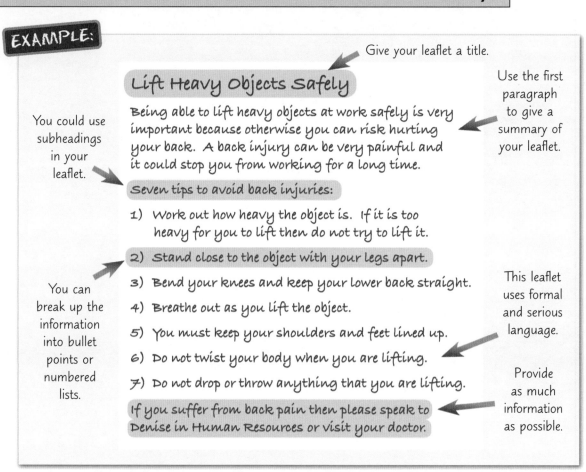

EXAMPLE:

Give your leaflet a title.

Lift Heavy Objects Safely

You could use subheadings in your leaflet.

Being able to lift heavy objects at work safely is very important because otherwise you can risk hurting your back. A back injury can be very painful and it could stop you from working for a long time.

Use the first paragraph to give a summary of your leaflet.

Seven tips to avoid back injuries:

1) Work out how heavy the object is. If it is too heavy for you to lift then do not try to lift it.

2) Stand close to the object with your legs apart.

You can break up the information into bullet points or numbered lists.

3) Bend your knees and keep your lower back straight.

4) Breathe out as you lift the object.

5) You must keep your shoulders and feet lined up.

6) Do not twist your body when you are lifting.

7) Do not drop or throw anything that you are lifting.

This leaflet uses formal and serious language.

If you suffer from back pain then please speak to Denise in Human Resources or visit your doctor.

Provide as much information as possible.

Practice Question

1) You receive the email below from someone you work with.

From: vikram.shah@officemail.co.uk
To: you@officemail.co.uk
Subject: New Employees Leaflet

Send

Hello

I'd like you to put together a leaflet which will encourage people to apply for a job at this company. I'd like you to provide as much information as possible about the office here, the area where we are located and the benefits of working for this company.

I look forward to seeing what you come up with.

All the best
Vikram

Write a leaflet which:

• tells people what the company you work for is like

• gives information about the area in which your company is located

• persuades people to apply for a job at your company

Use the space below to plan your answer. Write your answer on a separate piece of paper. Make sure your spelling, punctuation and grammar are correct.

Writing Persuasively

Persuasive writing convinces the reader to do something

1) You need to be **persuasive** in a lot of **different types** of writing.

2) If you're writing an **email** asking for **sponsorship**, then you need to be **persuasive**.

3) In a **letter** of **complaint** you might try to **persuade** the reader to give you a **refund**.

4) You might need to write **persuasively** to get someone to **take part** in an **activity**.

Explain why the reader should do what you want them to

To be persuasive you need to **give reasons why** someone should do something.

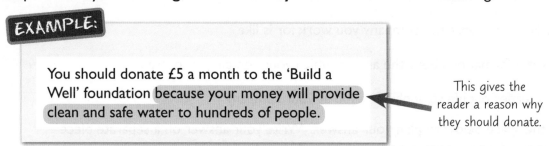

EXAMPLE:

You should donate £5 a month to the 'Build a Well' foundation because your money will provide clean and safe water to hundreds of people.

This gives the reader a reason why they should donate.

Persuasive writing makes the reader feel something

1) Use **descriptive words** in persuasive writing.

2) These descriptive words can make the reader **feel** a **certain emotion**.

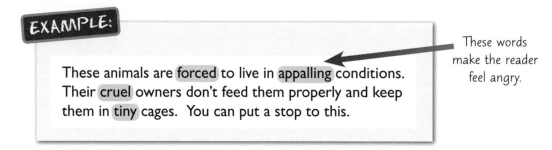

EXAMPLE:

These animals are forced to live in appalling conditions. Their cruel owners don't feed them properly and keep them in tiny cages. You can put a stop to this.

These words make the reader feel angry.

3) Using words like '**you**' and '**your**' makes a text **more persuasive**.

4) This is because it sounds like you are **talking directly** to the **reader**.

Practice Question

1) You want to enter the competition below.

A Deserved Break

Here at Relax Holidays, we're giving away a free 7-day holiday to Barbados to whoever we think really deserves a break. So, if you're someone who works really hard and has no time to relax, or someone who has gone through a tough patch and needs to get away from it all, get in touch. Write us a short letter, and give us plenty of reasons why you think you deserve a break. Who knows, you might get that break you deserve.

Contact us at: Relax Holidays, 4 Mill Street, Holloway, London, N7 7DE

Write a letter to persuade the staff at Relax Holidays to award you the free holiday. Remember to:

- give reasons why you should be chosen

- write persuasively

- lay out your letter correctly

Use the space below to plan your answer. Write your answer on a separate piece of paper. Make sure your spelling, punctuation and grammar are correct.

Writing About Your Opinions

Sometimes you'll need to give your opinion

1) You may be asked if you **agree** or **disagree** with something.

2) This means you need to give **your own opinion**.

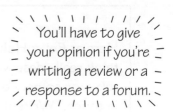
You'll have to give your opinion if you're writing a review or a response to a forum.

Give evidence to support your opinions

1) Your opinion **can't** be **right** or **wrong**...

2) ...but you have to **back up** your opinion with **evidence**.

EXAMPLE:

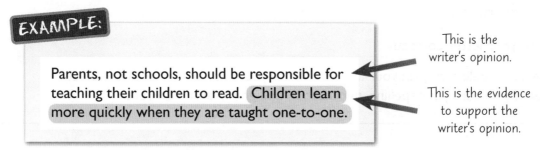

Parents, not schools, should be responsible for teaching their children to read. Children learn more quickly when they are taught one-to-one.

This is the writer's opinion.

This is the evidence to support the writer's opinion.

3) Your opinion will sound **more convincing** if it's supported by **evidence**.

You might find it difficult to pick your opinion

1) It's fine to **argue both sides** of an argument...

2) ...but you should try to reach a **conclusion**.

EXAMPLE:

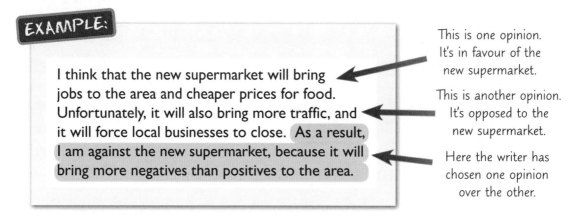

I think that the new supermarket will bring jobs to the area and cheaper prices for food. Unfortunately, it will also bring more traffic, and it will force local businesses to close. As a result, I am against the new supermarket, because it will bring more negatives than positives to the area.

This is one opinion. It's in favour of the new supermarket.

This is another opinion. It's opposed to the new supermarket.

Here the writer has chosen one opinion over the other.

3) Even if you **disagree** with someone, your language should be **polite** and **respectful**.

Practice Question

1) You read the comments below on an internet forum.

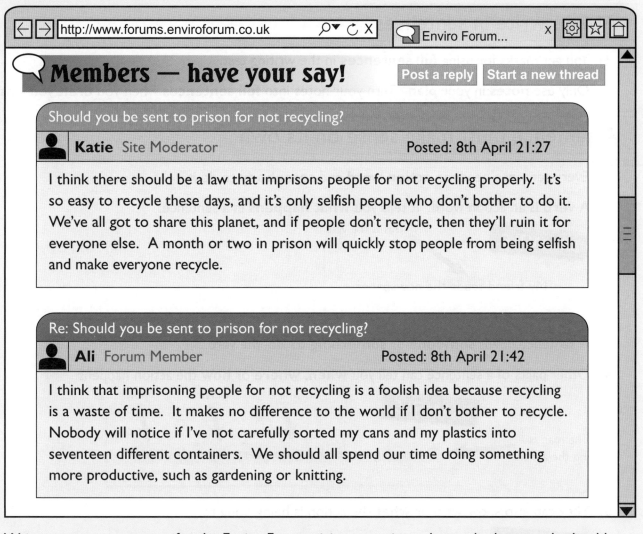

Write your own comment for the Enviro Forum giving your views about whether people should be sent to prison for not recycling. Do not just repeat what has already been said — try to come up with your own ideas. Use the space below to plan your answer. Make sure your spelling, punctuation and grammar are correct.

Using Sentences

Always write in sentences

1) You get marks for using **full sentences** in the writing test.

2) Only use **notes** in your **plan**. Turn your notes into **full sentences** when you **draft** your answer.

A sentence must make sense on its own

1) Every sentence needs an **action word** and **somebody** to do it.

2) A **verb** is an action word. It tells you **what happens** in a sentence.

EXAMPLE:

This is the verb.

My friend reads the newspaper.

3) A sentence needs **someone** or **something** to 'do' the verb.

4) Other parts of a sentence can tell you **when, where** or **how** the action happens.

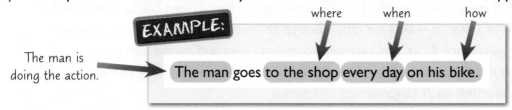

EXAMPLE:

where   when   how

The man is doing the action.

The man goes to the shop every day on his bike.

5) They can also show **who** or **what** the action is being done to.

EXAMPLE:

The visiting was 'done' to the neighbour.

I visited my neighbour.

Make sure your sentences are straight to the point

1) Make sure your sentences aren't **too long** or **confusing**.

2) If a sentence is too long, **split** it into **two shorter sentences**.

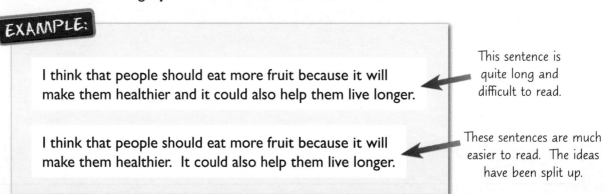

EXAMPLE:

I think that people should eat more fruit because it will make them healthier and it could also help them live longer.

This sentence is quite long and difficult to read.

I think that people should eat more fruit because it will make them healthier. It could also help them live longer.

These sentences are much easier to read. The ideas have been split up.

Practice Questions

1) Underline the **verb** in each sentence.

   a)   We arrived at the restaurant early.   d)   Everyone likes chocolate milkshakes.

   b)   I go to the gym every Thursday.   e)   She came to the party on her own.

   c)   The whole family wanted a new car.   f)   I work part-time in a bank.

2) Underline **who** or **what** is doing the action in each sentence.

   a)   Rabbits often eat garden plants.   d)   The supermarket is open all day.

   b)   I walked to the lake yesterday.   e)   Anita showed me a funny photo.

   c)   He always drinks tea with sugar.   f)   We are going to France next week.

3) Underline **when** the action happens in each sentence.

   a)   He went to work early.   d)   She goes swimming on Tuesdays.

   b)   Guinea pigs eat hay every day.   e)   My brother goes running in the mornings.

   c)   The shop closes at 6 pm.   f)   I'm going to Spain next week.

4) Underline **where** the action happens in each sentence.

   a)   We often go to an Italian restaurant.   d)   I visited the art gallery last week.

   b)   She loves travelling in Norway.   e)   My dog sleeps in the living room.

   c)   Polar bears live in the Arctic.   f)   They bought fruit from the shop.

5) Read these notes from a village noticeboard. Rewrite the notes in full sentences.

> cat missing yesterday
> small, long-haired, black and white
> last seen in garden
> if any information let owner know

....

....

....

....

....

Using Joining Words to Add Detail

Use joining words to make your writing sound better

Joining words link parts of sentences **together**.

EXAMPLE:

I enjoy shopping. I like clothes. ➡ I enjoy shopping because I like clothes.

Using 'because' joins the two sentences together and shows how they're connected.

'And', 'because' and 'so' add another point

Use '**and**', '**because**' or '**so**' to add **more detail** to a sentence.

1.

I like reading books and magazines.

2.

Amy is happy because she won the lottery.

'because' and 'so' introduce explanations.

3.

Jake is getting fit, so he goes jogging every night.

'But' and 'or' disagree with a point

1) Use '**but**' to **disagree** with something that's just been said.

EXAMPLE:

Oliver usually has toast for breakfast but today he had cereal.

2) Use '**or**' to give an **alternative**.

EXAMPLE:

We could go shopping tomorrow or we could go bowling.

Practice Questions

1) Choose 'and', 'or', 'so', 'because' or 'but' to complete these sentences.

   a) I will either buy a T-shirt .... some trousers from the shop.

   b) I can't come to the meeting today .... I have a dental appointment.

   c) I'm going to cut the cake into slices .... that everyone gets some.

   d) They would have come over .... they already had tickets for a play.

   e) He couldn't decide whether to wait for her .... leave without her.

   f) She's always loved baking cakes .... knitting.

   g) You can't put that glass there .... it will fall off and break.

   h) I got up very early .... that I could see the sunrise.

2) • Your friend has asked you to go to a restaurant for dinner on 2nd February and then go
     to a concert afterwards.
   • He has suggested you go for dinner at 7 pm so that you can get to the concert for 10 pm
     (when it starts).
   • You would like to go for dinner, but you have to pick your brother up from work at 10.30 pm.

   Write a short reply to your friend, explaining why you can only go for dinner.
   Try to use the joining words 'so', 'because' and 'but'. You don't need to worry about layout.

   ....

   ....

   ....

   ....

   ....

   ....

   ....

   ....

Using Joining Words to Link Ideas

Joining words can help structure your writing

Use **joining words** to link your **sentences** together to make **paragraphs**.

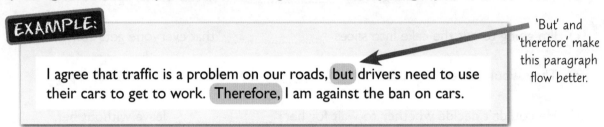

EXAMPLE:

> I agree that traffic is a problem on our roads, but drivers need to use their cars to get to work. Therefore, I am against the ban on cars.

'But' and 'therefore' make this paragraph flow better.

Use joining words to put your points in order

1) Use **'firstly'** to introduce your **most important point**.

EXAMPLE:

> Firstly, I think the most important issue is obesity...

'Firstly', 'secondly' and 'finally' are usually only used in formal texts.

2) Use **'secondly'** to make your **next point**.

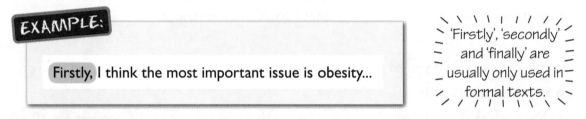

EXAMPLE:

> Secondly, another issue is P.E. in schools...

You could use 'in addition' or 'furthermore' instead of 'secondly'.

3) Use **'finally'** to round off your argument.

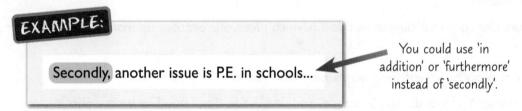

EXAMPLE:

> Finally, I want you to make school meals healthier...

You could use 'in conclusion' or 'therefore' instead of 'finally'.

Use 'however' and 'therefore' to develop your writing

1) Use **'therefore'** to explain a result.

2) **'However'** can be used to disagree with something that has just been said.

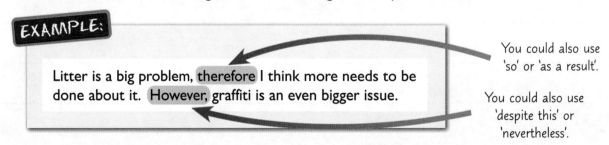

EXAMPLE:

> Litter is a big problem, therefore I think more needs to be done about it. However, graffiti is an even bigger issue.

You could also use 'so' or 'as a result'.

You could also use 'despite this' or 'nevertheless'.

Using Joining Words to Link Ideas

Use 'for example' to add an example

Use '**for example**' to back up your point.

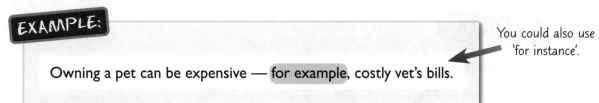

EXAMPLE:

Owning a pet can be expensive — for example, costly vet's bills.

You could also use 'for instance'.

Practice Questions

1) Choose 'therefore', 'for example' or 'however' to complete these sentences.

   a) I broke my leg, ... I couldn't play football.

   b) It was very rainy, ... it was still quite warm.

   c) I'm a really bad cook, ... I once set the oven on fire.

   d) The tyres need changing, ... the lorry isn't safe to drive.

   e) I want to go somewhere warm on holiday this year, ... Greece or Spain.

   f) He was angry when he got to work, ... he cheered up later in the day.

2) Use 'firstly', 'secondly', 'therefore', 'for example' and 'however' to complete this text.

   ...., the main argument for banning mobile phones is that they can be harmful.

   They can cause all sorts of problems, ..., if they are used while driving, they can

   lead to road traffic accidents.

   ...., mobile phones are bad for your health. Some reports suggest that

   texting could cause arthritis.

   ...., mobile phones have become an important part of everyday life, and they

   help people stay in touch with their friends and family.

   ...., I think we should think carefully about how much we use mobile phones,

   and try to avoid using them where possible.

Using Different Verb Tenses

A verb is a doing or being word

Verbs tell you what something **does** or **is**.

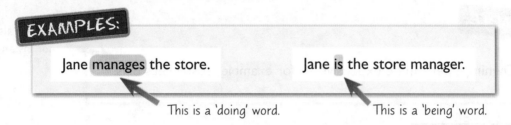

EXAMPLES:

Jane manages the store.   Jane is the store manager.

This is a 'doing' word.   This is a 'being' word.

Use the present tense to say what is happening now

Most verbs in the **present tense** follow the same **verb pattern**:

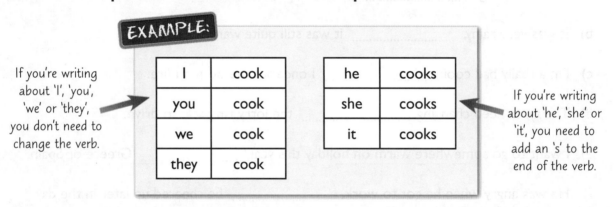

EXAMPLE:

If you're writing about 'I', 'you', 'we' or 'they', you don't need to change the verb.

I	cook
you	cook
we	cook
they	cook

he	cooks
she	cooks
it	cooks

If you're writing about 'he', 'she' or 'it', you need to add an 's' to the end of the verb.

How you change the verb depends on who is doing it

Use the **verb pattern** to work out the correct ending.

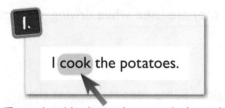

1.

I cook the potatoes.

The verb table shows that you don't need to change the verb when you're writing about 'I'.

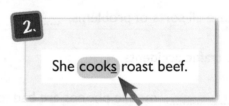

2.

She cooks roast beef.

You need to add an 's' to the verb because you're talking about 'she'.

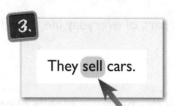

3.

They sell cars.

You don't need to change the verb when you're writing about 'they'.

4.

It sells groceries.

You need to add an 's' to the verb because you're talking about 'it'.

Using Different Verb Tenses

Use the past tense to say what has already happened

1) Most verbs need '**ed**' at the end to make them into the past tense.

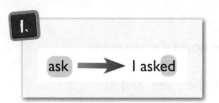

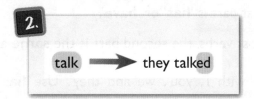

2) If the verb already ends in '**e**', just add a '**d**' to the end.

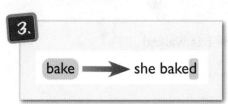

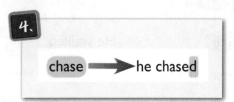

Not all past tense verbs add 'ed'

1) Some common verbs **act differently**.

Use 'was' for 'I', 'he', 'she' and 'it'.
Use 'were' for 'you', 'we' and 'they'.

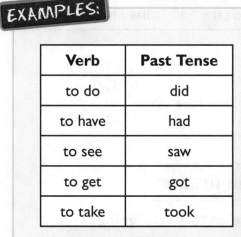

Verb	Past Tense
to do	did
to have	had
to see	saw
to get	got
to take	took

Verb	Past Tense
to be	was / were
to go	went
to make	made
to come	came
to think	thought

These are just a few examples. There are other verbs that act differently too.

2) Some verbs **don't change** at all in the past tense.

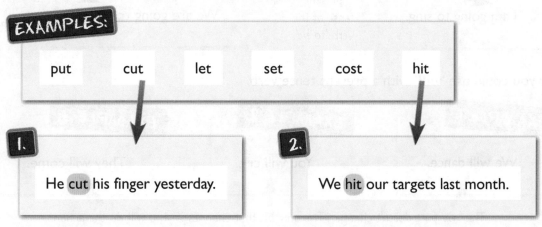

| put | cut | let | set | cost | hit |

1.
He cut his finger yesterday.

2.
We hit our targets last month.

Using Different Verb Tenses

Use the past tense with 'have' to talk about recent actions

1) The past tense with 'have' uses **two parts**.

   - The first part is **'has'** or **'have'**.

   - For most verbs, the second part is the **same** as the normal past tense.

2) Use **'have'** with 'I', 'you', 'we' and 'they'. Use **'has'** with 'he', 'she' and 'it'.

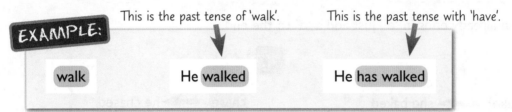

EXAMPLE:

This is the past tense of 'walk'.　　This is the past tense with 'have'.

walk　　　　He walked　　　　He has walked

3) For some verbs, the second part is **different** to the normal past tense.

Verb	Past with 'have'	Verb	Past with 'have'
to do	has / have done	to go	has / have gone
to be	has / have been	to write	has / have written
to see	has / have seen	to take	has / have taken

EXAMPLE:

take　　　　They took　　　　They have taken

There are two ways to talk about the future

1) Talk about future actions by using **'am'**, **'is'** or **'are'** and the verb **'going'**.

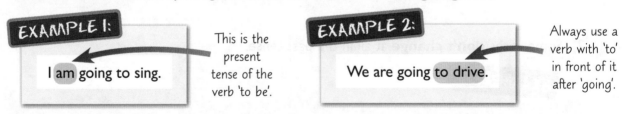

EXAMPLE 1:

I am going to sing.

This is the present tense of the verb 'to be'.

EXAMPLE 2:

We are going to drive.

Always use a verb with 'to' in front of it after 'going'.

2) Or you could use **'will'** with a present tense verb.

EXAMPLE 1:

We will dance.

EXAMPLE 2:

You will cry.

EXAMPLE 3:

They will come.

The 'will' part doesn't change. The only bit that changes is who will do the action.

Practice Questions

1) Rewrite each sentence in the past tense. Use the normal past tense (not with 'have').

   a) Sarah walks to the park.

   ....

   b) She has pasta for dinner.

   ....

   c) I see a field of sheep on the way to work.

   ....

   d) He asks her for a lift to the station.

   ....

   e) We go to the festival.

   ....

2) Circle the correct verb to complete each sentence.

   a) Andy **writes / write** a letter.   e) They often **goes / go** out on Friday.

   b) Becky always **wear / wears** dresses.   f) I **play / plays** the piano.

   c) I **have / has** two dogs and a cat.   g) Abby never **does / do** any exercise.

   d) Their course **was / were** very difficult. h) We always **bake / bakes** cakes.

3) Rewrite these sentences in the future tense. Use the future tense with 'will'.

   a) I made an apple crumble.

   ....

   b) He came to football practice.

   ....

   c) They were angry.

   ....

   d) The horse ate lots of grass.

   ....

Common Mistakes With Verbs

A verb must agree with the person doing the action

1) Check **who** is doing the action to work out if the **verb** should **change**.

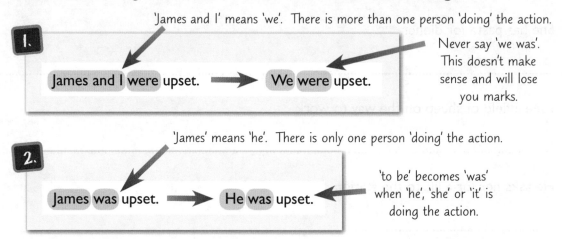

2) To say 'there **is**' or 'there **are**', use the right '**being**' word to match the person.

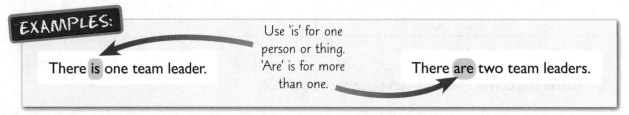

'Been' and 'done' always go with 'have' or 'has'

Always use '**have**' or '**has**' when you write 'been' or 'done'.

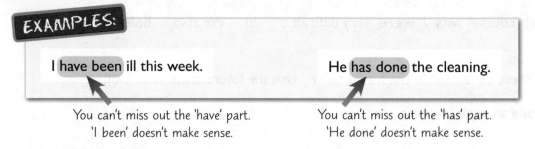

Don't confuse 'could've' with 'could of'

1) Always write '**could have**'. Never write 'could of' because it doesn't mean anything.

2) It's the same for '**might have**' and '**should have**'.

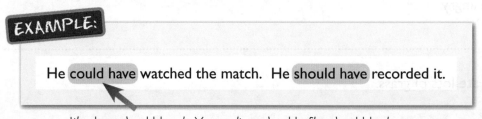

Common Mistakes With Verbs

'Don't' means 'do not' and 'doesn't' means 'does not'

1) Use '**don't**' with 'I', 'you', 'we' and 'they'.

2) Use '**doesn't**' with 'he', 'she' and 'it'.

I don't want to leave.

This is short for 'I do not'.

He doesn't drink coffee.

This is short for 'He does not'.

Practice Questions

1) A verb in each of these sentences is wrong. Rewrite the sentence without any mistakes.

a) There are one cat.

....

b) James don't work on Mondays.

....

c) We was on the train to London.

....

d) The men have being on holiday.

....

2) Rewrite each sentence so that it makes sense.

a) She might of broken her leg.

....

b) They could of cleaned the house.

....

c) I should of gone with him to the bank.

....

Punctuating Sentences

Every sentence should start with a capital letter

1) **Every sentence** should begin with a **capital letter**.

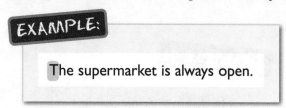

> The supermarket is always open.

2) Some words begin with a **capital letter** even in the **middle** of a sentence.

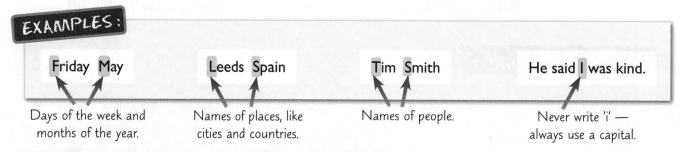

EXAMPLES:

Friday May

Leeds Spain

Tim Smith

He said I was kind.

Days of the week and months of the year.

Names of places, like cities and countries.

Names of people.

Never write 'i' — always use a capital.

Most sentences end with a full stop

1) Use a **full stop** to show that your sentence has **finished**.

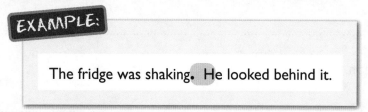

> The fridge was shaking. He looked behind it.

2) Use an **exclamation mark** if you're saying something really **amazing**.

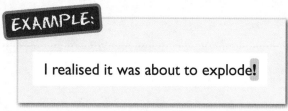

> I realised it was about to explode!

3) Try not to use **too many** exclamation marks. If you're not sure, use a **full stop instead**.

Questions end with question marks

1) A question should **start** with a **capital letter**...

2) ...but it should end with a **question mark** instead of a full stop.

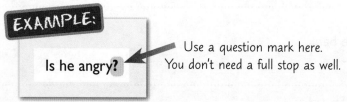

EXAMPLE:

Is he angry?

Use a question mark here. You don't need a full stop as well.

Practice Questions

1) Use capital letters and full stops to write these sentences correctly.
   You might need to write two sentences instead of one.

   a) the trees in scotland were about 50 ft high

   ....

   b) on monday he slipped and fell over crossing the river

   ....

   c) hiking isn't much fun with the wrong shoes

   ....

   d) I don't know where he is he might have gone shopping in manchester

   ....

   ....

   e) polar bears are known to be violent i hope we don't see one

   ....

   ....

   f) he advertised his sofa in the newspaper he sold it for £100

   ....

   ....

2) Use a full stop, an exclamation mark or a question mark to end each sentence correctly.

   a)   Why are there so many horror films out at the moment...

   b)   It turned out that his own brother was the villain... That surprised everyone...

   c)   We went to see the football last night... The second half was amazing...

   d)   That's awful... We should do something about it...

   e)   How can you like that band... I don't think they're any good...

   f)   They've sold more records this year than last year... How have they done that...

   g)   There were slugs on the garden path... One crawled in my shoe...

Using Commas

Commas separate things in a list

1) **Commas** can **break up lists** of **three** or **more** things.

2) Put a **comma** after **each thing** in the list.

3) Between the **last two things** you **don't** need a **comma**. Use **'and'** or **'or'** instead.

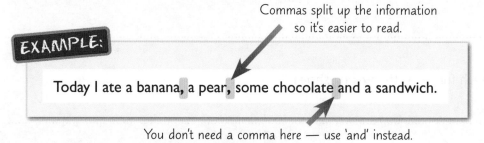

Commas split up the information so it's easier to read.

EXAMPLE:

Today I ate a banana, a pear, some chocolate and a sandwich.

You don't need a comma here — use 'and' instead.

Commas can join two points

1) **Two sentences** can be **joined** using a **joining word** and a **comma**.

2) **Joining words** are words like **'and'**, **'but'** and **'so'**.

3) The comma is added **before** the joining word to show where the new sentence **begins**.

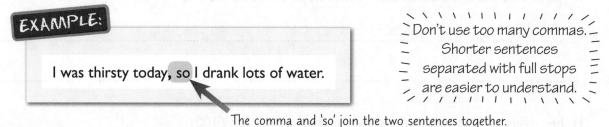

EXAMPLE:

I was thirsty today, so I drank lots of water.

The comma and 'so' join the two sentences together.

Don't use too many commas. Shorter sentences separated with full stops are easier to understand.

Commas can separate extra information

1) **Extra information** in a sentence can be **separated** using **commas**.

2) Extra information adds **detail**, but you **don't need it** for the sentence to **make sense**.

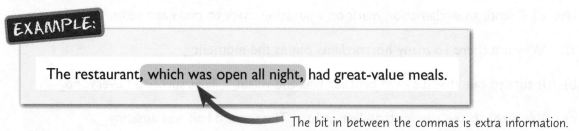

EXAMPLE:

The restaurant, which was open all night, had great-value meals.

The bit in between the commas is extra information.

3) To check if you've used these commas correctly, **remove** the words **inside** the **commas**.

EXAMPLE:

The restaurant had great-value meals.

If the sentence still makes sense, then you're using them correctly.

Using Commas

Extra information can begin or end a sentence

1) Sometimes the extra information can come at the **start** of a sentence.

2) In this case, you only need to use **one** comma rather than **two**.

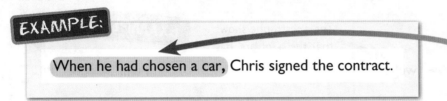

EXAMPLE:

When he had chosen a car, Chris signed the contract.

The first bit of the sentence is extra information — it's separated from the second part with a comma.

3) The extra information could also come at the **end** of the sentence.

4) In this case, you **don't** need to use a comma to separate the two parts of the sentence.

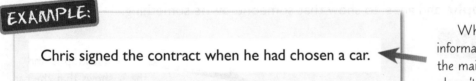

EXAMPLE:

Chris signed the contract when he had chosen a car.

When the extra information comes **after** the main information, it doesn't need a comma.

Practice Questions

1) Correct these sentences by putting commas in the right places.

a) You need to add cinnamon nutmeg and vanilla to the cake mix.

b) The cat which looked like a stray was very friendly.

c) James injured his shoulder so he couldn't go bowling.

d) The bookshop sells biographies thrillers and romances.

e) Although the cinema was full it was completely silent.

f) Would you like chocolate chip vanilla or strawberry ice cream?

g) They were going to go to the concert but they missed the bus.

h) Alex Johns who was my best man never made it to the wedding.

i) Our team reached the finals so we went out to celebrate.

j) I want chopped onions lettuce peppers and tomatoes in my sandwich.

k) Jim and Maher were going to London but they changed their minds.

l) The flat-pack table which had instructions with it was easy to build.

m) The café which sold lots of different types of tea was very popular.

Using Apostrophes

Apostrophes show that letters are missing

1) An **apostrophe** looks like this — **'** .

2) Apostrophes show where letters have been **removed**.

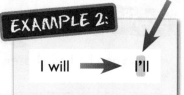

EXAMPLE 1:

we are ➡ we're

The apostrophe shows that the 'a' of 'are' has been removed.

EXAMPLE 2:

I will ➡ I'll

The apostrophe shows that the 'w' and 'i' of 'will' have been removed.

Apostrophes show something belongs to someone

Use an **apostrophe** and an **'s'** to show that someone **owns** something.

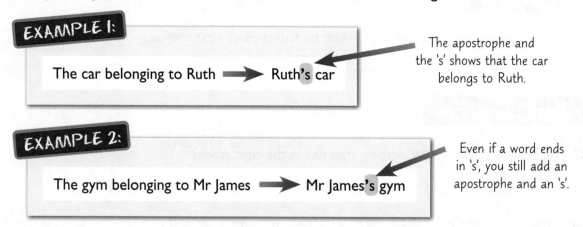

EXAMPLE 1:

The car belonging to Ruth ➡ Ruth's car

The apostrophe and the 's' shows that the car belongs to Ruth.

EXAMPLE 2:

The gym belonging to Mr James ➡ Mr James's gym

Even if a word ends in 's', you still add an apostrophe and an 's'.

'it's' and 'its' mean different things

1) **'It's'** with an apostrophe means 'it is' or 'it has'.

2) The **apostrophe** shows that there are **letters missing**.

EXAMPLE:

It is time for lunch. ➡ It's time for lunch.

The apostrophe shows that the 'i' is missing from 'is'.

3) **'Its'** without an apostrophe means 'belonging to it'.

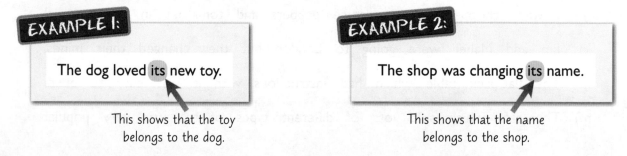

EXAMPLE 1:

The dog loved its new toy.

This shows that the toy belongs to the dog.

EXAMPLE 2:

The shop was changing its name.

This shows that the name belongs to the shop.

Using Apostrophes

Don't use apostrophes for plurals

Never use an apostrophe to show that there's **more than one** of something.

This is wrong.

 **EXAMPLES:**

| two phones | NOT | two phone's | | some ducks | NOT | some duck's |

Practice Questions

1) Shorten these phrases by putting apostrophes in the correct places.

   a) have not ....

   b) you will ....

   c) I would ....

   d) could not ....

   e) you are ....

   f) did not ....

2) Rewrite these sentences using apostrophes to show who owns what.

   a) the car park belonging to the office

   ....

   b) the sweets belonging to the child

   ....

   c) the fingerprints belonging to the burglar

   ....

   d) the uniform belonging to the nurse

   ....

3) Circle the correct word to use in each sentence.

   a) **It's / Its** not surprising that **it's / its** fallen over.

   b) The team won **it's / its** final match. **It's / Its** unbelievable!

   c) **It's / Its** so nice to see your cat and **it's / its** kittens.

Using Inverted Commas

There are two types of inverted commas

1) **Single inverted commas** look a bit like apostrophes **' '**. They always come in **pairs**.

2) One goes at the **beginning** of a word or phrase, the other goes at the **end**.

EXAMPLES:

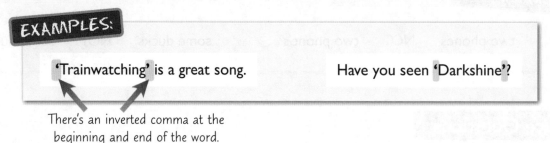

'Trainwatching' is a great song.   Have you seen 'Darkshine'?

There's an inverted comma at the
beginning and end of the word.

3) **Double inverted commas** look like a **pair** of single inverted commas — **" "**.

EXAMPLES:

"I'll come to yours at 7 pm."   "Stop right there," she said.

Like single inverted commas, double inverted commas always come in twos.

Single inverted commas are used for titles

Titles of things, for example books or films, usually go inside **single inverted commas**.

EXAMPLES:

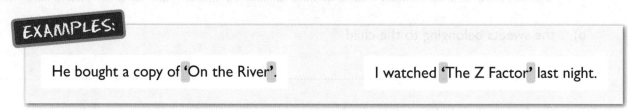

He bought a copy of 'On the River'.   I watched 'The Z Factor' last night.

Double inverted commas are used to quote

Double inverted commas go around the **actual words** that **someone says**.

EXAMPLES:

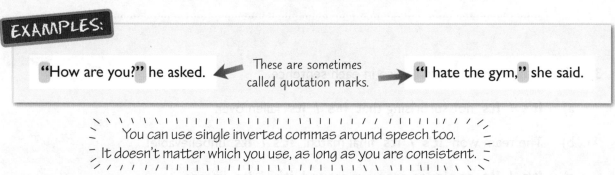

"How are you?" he asked.   ← These are sometimes
called quotation marks. →   "I hate the gym," she said.

You can use single inverted commas around speech too.
It doesn't matter which you use, as long as you are consistent.

Practice Questions

1) Correct these sentences by putting single inverted commas in the right places.

a) Have you read his new book, Glimpsing Heaven ?

b) It's the first time I've ever seen The Woman in Blue .

c) The Sparkshire Herald is full of interesting articles .

d) Come Dance With Me is my favourite TV programme .

2) Rewrite these sentences using double inverted commas in the correct places.

a) Happy Birthday! we all shouted together.

b) Get out and never come back! he shouted at us.

c) Have you got the time? the old man asked.

d) She said, I want you to start calling earlier in the evening.

e) I've forgotten my work boots again, complained Craig.

f) The supporters shouted, Come on Hadych! You can do it!

Section Four — Using Correct Punctuation

Spelling Tricks

The 'i' before 'e' rule

1) 'i' and 'e' often appear **next to each other** in a word.

2) This means it can be **tricky** to **remember** which comes **first**.

3) Use the **'i' before 'e' rule** to help:

'i' before 'e' except after 'c', but only when it rhymes with 'bee'.

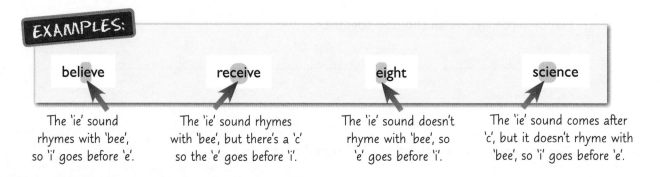

EXAMPLES:

believe	receive	eight	science
The 'ie' sound rhymes with 'bee', so 'i' goes before 'e'.	The 'ie' sound rhymes with 'bee', but there's a 'c' so the 'e' goes before 'i'.	The 'ie' sound doesn't rhyme with 'bee', so 'e' goes before 'i'.	The 'ie' sound comes after 'c', but it doesn't rhyme with 'bee', so 'i' goes before 'e'.

A few words don't follow the rule

Watch out for these **tricky examples**.

If you're not sure about the spelling of a word, check your dictionary.

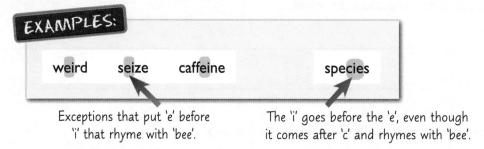

EXAMPLES:

weird   seize   caffeine   species

Exceptions that put 'e' before 'i' that rhyme with 'bee'.

The 'i' goes before the 'e', even though it comes after 'c' and rhymes with 'bee'.

Use memorable phrases to help you spell tricky words

Make up **sentences** or **phrases** to remind you how words are spelt.

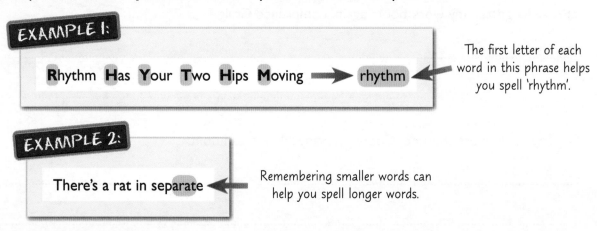

EXAMPLE 1:

Rhythm **H**as **Y**our **T**wo **H**ips **M**oving ⟶ rhythm

The first letter of each word in this phrase helps you spell 'rhythm'.

EXAMPLE 2:

There's a rat in separate ⟵ Remembering smaller words can help you spell longer words.

Practice Questions

1) Rewrite each word so that it is spelt correctly. Some words may already be correct.

a) recieve   ....

d) fierce   ....

b) science   ....

e) freind   ....

c) acheive   ....

f) wierd   ....

2) Think of four words that you find tricky to spell. Look up the spelling of each word in a dictionary and write it in the box. Think of a phrase that will help you remember how to spell it.

....

....

....

....

....

....

....

....

Making Plurals

Plural means 'more than one'

1) To make most words **plural**, you add an '**s**' on the **end**.

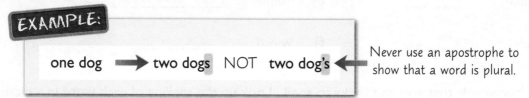

EXAMPLE:

one dog ➡ two dogs   NOT   two dog's

Never use an apostrophe to show that a word is plural.

2) If a word **ends** with '**ch**', '**x**', '**s**', '**sh**' or '**z**', put '**es**' on the **end** to make it plural.

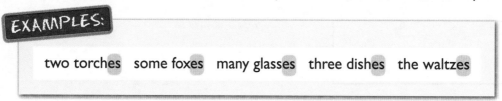

EXAMPLES:

two torches   some foxes   many glasses   three dishes   the waltzes

Words ending with 'y' have different rules

1) Some words end with a **vowel** ('a', 'e', 'i', 'o' or 'u') and then a '**y**'.

2) To make these words **plural**, put an '**s**' on the end. For example, 'tray' becomes 'tray**s**'.

3) If a word ends in a **consonant** and then a '**y**', change the '**y**' to an '**i**' and then add '**es**' on the **end**.

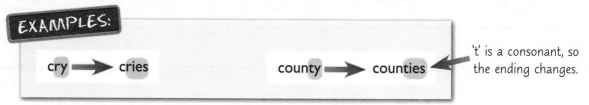

EXAMPLES:

cry ➡ cries   county ➡ counties

't' is a consonant, so the ending changes.

Words ending with 'f' or 'fe' need a 'v'

1) To make words ending with '**f**' **plural**, change the '**f**' to a '**v**' and add '**es**'.

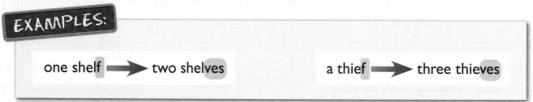

EXAMPLES:

one shelf ➡ two shelves   a thief ➡ three thieves

2) To make words ending with '**fe**' **plural**, change the '**f**' to a '**v**' and add '**s**'.

EXAMPLES:

one wife ➡ two wives   a knife ➡ three knives

Making Plurals

Some words don't follow a pattern

EXAMPLES:

1. To make some words **plural**, you have to change the **spelling** of the word.

tooth ➡ teeth   woman ➡ women   mouse ➡ mice

2. Some words **don't change at all**.

fish   deer   sheep

> You would always say 'two sheep', never 'two sheeps'.

Practice Questions

1) Write the plural of each word.

a) cinema ....   e) baby ....

b) Friday ....   f) half ....

c) brush ....   g) reindeer ....

d) journey ....   h) monkey ....

2) Rewrite each of these sentences with the correct plurals.

a) The boyes ate all the peachs.

....

b) The puppys played in the leafs.

....

c) Spys always carry knifes.

....

d) The branchs were burnt to ashs.

....

Adding Prefixes and Suffixes

Prefixes and suffixes are used to make new words

1) **Prefixes** are **letters** that are added to the **start** of words.

2) When you add a **prefix**, it **changes** the **meaning** of the word.

EXAMPLES:

un + well ➞ unwell   dis + agree ➞ disagree

3) **Suffixes** are letters that are added to the **end** of words.

4) When you add a **suffix**, it also **changes** the **meaning** of the word.

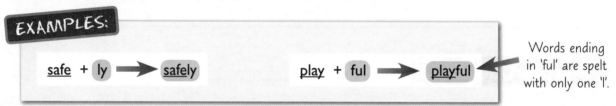

EXAMPLES:

safe + ly ➞ safely   play + ful ➞ playful

Words ending in 'ful' are spelt with only one 'l'.

Adding a prefix doesn't change the spelling

If you add a **prefix** to a word, the **spelling** of the **word stays the same**.

The spelling of the prefix and the word don't change.

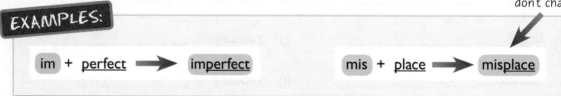

EXAMPLES:

im + perfect ➞ imperfect   mis + place ➞ misplace

Adding a suffix might change the spelling

1) If you add a **suffix** to a word, sometimes the spelling **changes**.

2) If a word ends in an 'e' and the **first letter** of the suffix is a **vowel**, you **drop** the 'e'.

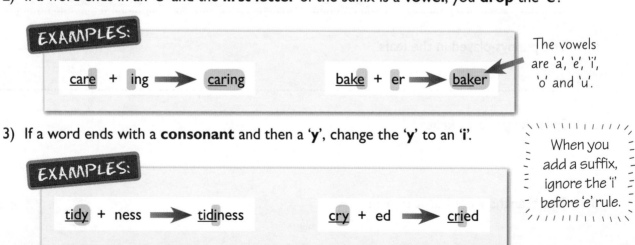

EXAMPLES:

care + ing ➞ caring   bake + er ➞ baker

The vowels are 'a', 'e', 'i', 'o' and 'u'.

3) If a word ends with a **consonant** and then a **'y'**, change the **'y'** to an **'i'**.

EXAMPLES:

tidy + ness ➞ tidiness   cry + ed ➞ cried

When you add a suffix, ignore the 'i' before 'e' rule.

Adding Prefixes and Suffixes

The C-V-C rule tells you when to double letters

1) If you're adding a **suffix** that begins with a **vowel**, you can use the **C-V-C rule**.

2) For most words, if the last three letters go **consonant - vowel - consonant (C-V-C)**...

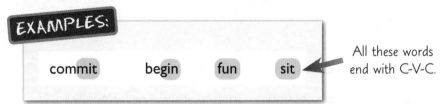

EXAMPLES:

commit   begin   fun   sit   ← All these words end with C-V-C.

3) ...you **double** the **last letter** when you add the **suffix**.

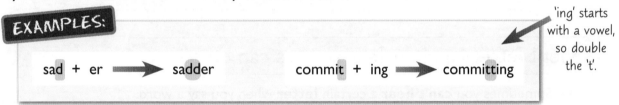

EXAMPLES:

sad + er ➝ sadder   commit + ing ➝ committing

'ing' starts with a vowel, so double the 't'.

4) If the **first letter** of the **suffix** is a **consonant**, you **don't** double the last letter.

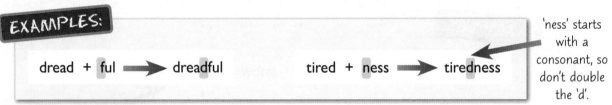

EXAMPLES:

dread + ful ➝ dreadful   tired + ness ➝ tiredness

'ness' starts with a consonant, so don't double the 'd'.

Practice Questions

1) Rewrite these words so they are spelt correctly. Some words may already be correct.

a) stopper   ....   d) repplay   ....

b) hopefull   ....   e) beautyful   ....

c) lovely   ....   f) misslead   ....

2) Rewrite each of these sentences and correct the mistakes.

a) He tryed to help the joger.

    ....

b) She was fameous for her kinddness.

    ....

c) I am puting this sillyness behind me.

    ....

Common Spelling Mistakes

Words with double letters can be hard to spell

1) It's tricky to spell words with **double letters** because you **can't hear them** when they're said.

2) **Learn** how to spell these **common** words with **double letters**.

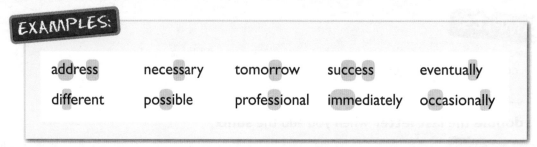

EXAMPLES:

address	necessary	tomorrow	success	eventually
different	possible	professional	immediately	occasionally

Silent letters and unclear sounds can be tricky

1) Sometimes you **can't hear** a certain **letter** when you say a word.

2) These are known as **silent letters**.

EXAMPLES:

when   which   write   whole   know   could   before   doubt

Make sure you learn all these tricky spellings.

3) Sometimes the **sound** in a word **isn't clear**.

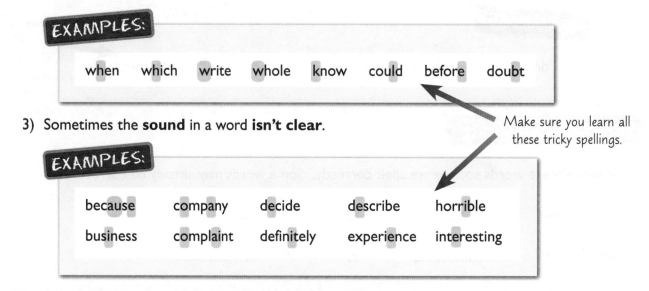

EXAMPLES:

because	company	decide	describe	horrible
business	complaint	definitely	experience	interesting

Make sure you're using the right word

1) '**A lot**' means '**many**', always write it as **two separate** words. '**Alot**' is **not** a real word.

2) '**Thank you**' is always written as **two words**.

3) '**As well**' is always written as two separate words. '**Aswell**' is **not** a real word.

4) '**Maybe**' means '**perhaps**'. '**May be**' means '**might be**'.

If you can swap in 'might be', then you're using the right version of 'may be'.

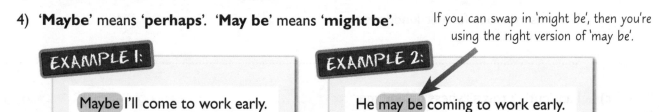

EXAMPLE 1:

Maybe I'll come to work early.

EXAMPLE 2:

He may be coming to work early.

Practice Questions

1) Each of these sentences has two mistakes. Correct the mistakes and rewrite the sentence.

a) He will deside where to go tommorow.

....

b) Wich hotel have you stayed at befor?

....

c) The hole thing was diferent this time.

....

d) Do you know wen you shud call back?

....

e) May be it's just not posible.

....

f) What is the adress of that shipping cumpany?

....

g) My experiance has been horibble.

....

h) You should now how to act proffesionally.

....

i) Thankyou for dealing with my complint.

....

j) I will definately use your busness again.

....

k) It maybe a leak, but I dout it.

....

l) Is it neccesary to do this imediately?

....

Commonly Confused Words

'Their', 'they're' and 'there' are all different

1) **'Their'** means 'belonging to them'.

> Their flat has two bedrooms.
>
> He took their warning seriously.

2) **'They're'** means 'they are'.

> They're living in a two-bed flat.
>
> They're giving him a warning.

If you can replace 'they're' with 'they are', and the sentence makes sense, then it's right.

3) **'There'** is used to talk about a **location**...

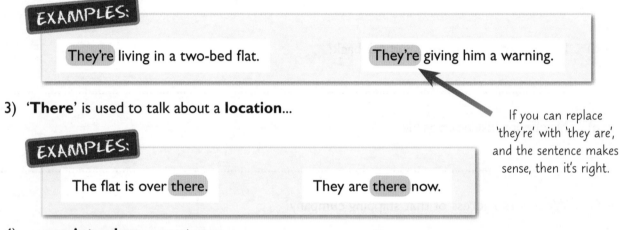

> The flat is over there.
>
> They are there now.

4) ...or to **introduce a sentence**.

> There is no reason to give him a warning.
>
> There are two choices.

Learn how to use 'to' and 'too'

1) **'To'** can mean 'towards' or it can be part of a **verb**.

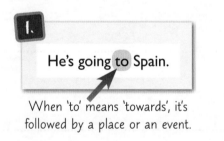

1. He's going to Spain.

When 'to' means 'towards', it's followed by a place or an event.

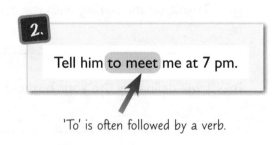

2. Tell him to meet me at 7 pm.

'To' is often followed by a verb.

2) **'Too'** can mean 'too much' or it can mean 'also'.

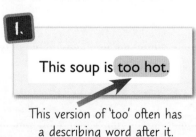

1. This soup is too hot.

This version of 'too' often has a describing word after it.

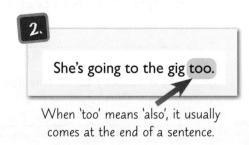

2. She's going to the gig too.

When 'too' means 'also', it usually comes at the end of a sentence.

Commonly Confused Words

'Your' and 'you're' mean different things

1) **'You're'** means 'you are'.

   If you can replace 'you're' with 'you are' and the sentence makes sense, then it's the right word.

   EXAMPLE 1:

   You're working twice this week.

2) **'Your'** means 'belonging to you'.

   EXAMPLE 2:

   Keep your uniform in your locker.

   The uniform belongs to you.

Don't confuse 'of' and 'off'

1) **'Off'** can mean 'not on'. **'Off'** can also mean 'away (from)'.

   EXAMPLES:

   Turn the lights off.

   I took Monday off work.

2) **'Of'** is a **linking word**. It **joins parts** of a sentence **together**.

   EXAMPLE:

   My wardrobe is full of clothes I don't wear.

'Are' and 'our' sound alike

EXAMPLES:

1. **'Are'** is a **verb** (doing word).

   We are paid every Friday.

   Are we going out tonight?

2. **'Our'** means 'belonging to us'.

   Our house is near the church.

   It's our favourite song.

Commonly Confused Words

'Been' and 'being' can sound the same

1) **'Been'** only ever comes after the words **'have'**, **'has'** or **'had'**.

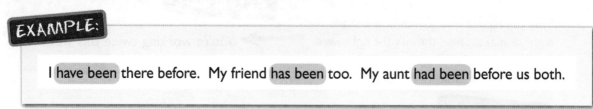

> EXAMPLE:
>
> I have been there before. My friend has been too. My aunt had been before us both.

2) **'Being'** comes after **'am'**, **'are'**, **'were'** or **'was'**.

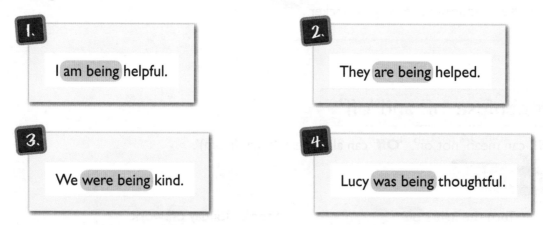

1. I am being helpful.

2. They are being helped.

3. We were being kind.

4. Lucy was being thoughtful.

'Bought' and 'brought' mean different things

'Brought' is the past tense of **'bring'**. **'Bought'** is the past tense of **'buy'**.

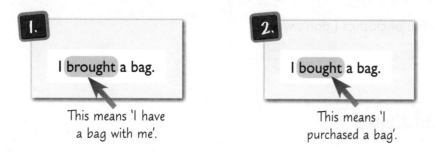

1. I brought a bag.

This means 'I have a bag with me'.

2. I bought a bag.

This means 'I purchased a bag'.

Teach and learn are opposites

1) You **teach** information **to** someone else.

2) You **learn** information **from** someone else.

> EXAMPLES:
>
> I teach Italian to my mother.   My mother learns Italian from me.

Practice Questions

1) Circle the correct word to use in each sentence.

   a) **Their / There** is no way to get **off / of** this bus early.

   b) **Are / Our** there **too / to** many people on board?

   c) I hope **you're / your** joking when you say **you're / your** going to buy a snake.

   d) **Their / They're** going to go **to / too** bed.

   e) He was **being / been** careless with **you're / your** car.

   f) Can you **learn / teach** me how to use **our / are** dishwasher?

2) Each of these sentences has two mistakes. Correct the mistakes and rewrite the sentence.

   a) They bought they're dog into work.

   ....

   b) There going to far this time.

   ....

   c) She wants to learn her son how too be polite.

   ....

   d) I think your tired off long hours.

   ....

   e) I want too teach cooking from an expert.

   ....

   f) Toby's being to the gym. Have you been going their too?

   ....

   g) I brought it from that new shop over their.

   ....

   h) Are you're children been naughty?

   ....

   i) Their is the cake I bought into work.

   ....

Section Five — Using Correct Spelling

Writing Test Advice

Always write a plan before you begin

If you're doing your test onscreen, you can still use a pen and paper to jot down rough work.

1) Writing a **plan** will help you put your ideas in the **right order**.

2) You will get marks if your answer has a **clear beginning**, **middle** and **end**.

3) If you're given a **text** or some **bullet points**, use information from them in your plan.

EXAMPLE:

You are taking part in a half-marathon for a children's charity.
Write an email persuading your co-workers to sponsor you.

You should include:

- When the half-marathon is taking place.

- Why and how your co-workers should sponsor you.

It might be helpful to write about the bullet points in the order they are given.

---

4) You might need to **make up** some details — for example, a business name.

5) If you **make up any details**, be **sensible** and make sure they add something **useful**.

6) Use any **similar experiences** you've had to make your writing more **believable**.

You get marked on spelling, punctuation and grammar

1) In the writing test, **correct spelling**, **punctuation** and **grammar** is worth a lot of marks.

2) **Never** use **text speak** even if you're asked to write an informal text.

3) If you're **copying** a word that's used in a source, make sure you spell it **correctly**.

4) If you're doing your test on paper, make sure your **handwriting is clear**.
   If it can't be read, you could **lose marks**.

Make sure you do what the question asks

1) Make sure you **only** include things that **answer the question**.

2) Leave yourself enough time to do **both parts** of the writing task.

3) Spend a few minutes **checking** through your work at the end.

4) Don't worry if you spot some **mistakes** — just try to correct them **carefully**.

5) Aim for between **200 and 300 words** for each text in the writing test.

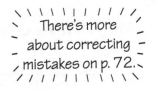

There's more about correcting mistakes on p. 72.

Exercise A — Thank You Letter

You are a member of the car breakdown service shown below.

Car Mechanics Club

- Membership is only £24.99 a year
- We fix 90% of cars on the roadside
- We will be with you and your car within 45 minutes
- We operate 24 hours a day
- Our mechanics are friendly and polite

Address: Car Mechanics Club, 27 Elvet Road,
Swindon, Wiltshire, SN1 3LD

Your car broke down last week. The Car Mechanics Club sent a mechanic to help you. You were impressed with the service you received, and you want to write a letter to thank the car breakdown service.

You should include:

- An explanation of your breakdown.

- Why you were impressed by the service provided by the Car Mechanics Club.

Remember to:

- Plan your answer.

- Use full sentences and paragraphs. You will be marked on spelling, punctuation and grammar.

- Set your letter out correctly.

You have 25 minutes to complete this exercise. You may use a dictionary.
Write your answer on a separate piece of paper.

(15 marks)

Plan your answer here:

Exercise B — Email to Sportswoman

You are the events organiser for the charity shown below.

Healthy Hearts Trust

Healthy Hearts is a charity committed to helping people fight heart disease. We were founded in 1986 with the aim of encouraging healthy living and reducing heart disease. We raise money through a number of different activities including sponsored fun runs, raffles and charity dinners. The charity has raised money to buy equipment at local hospitals and it has provided life-saving advice to people about how to keep their hearts healthy.

You read a newspaper article about a sportswoman called Louise Fitzgerald who wants to do more to help promote local charities. Write an email persuading her to take part in a charity event you are organising. You can contact her at: louise.fitzgerald@sportmail.co.uk

Remember to:

• Plan your answer.

• Use full sentences and paragraphs. You will be marked on spelling, punctuation and grammar.

• Set your email out correctly.

You have 25 minutes to complete this exercise. You may use a dictionary.
Write your answer on a separate piece of paper.

(15 marks)

> Plan your answer here:

Exercise C — Art Competition Article

You work for a magazine that promotes local art. You receive the following email from the editor.

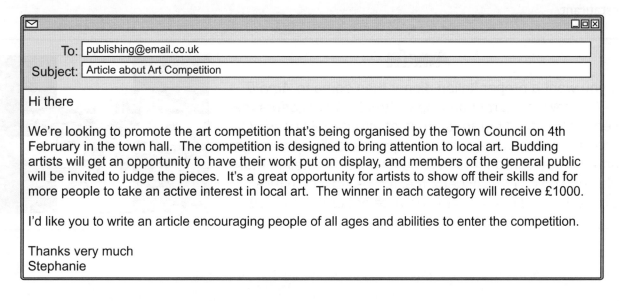

To: publishing@email.co.uk

Subject: Article about Art Competition

Hi there

We're looking to promote the art competition that's being organised by the Town Council on 4th February in the town hall. The competition is designed to bring attention to local art. Budding artists will get an opportunity to have their work put on display, and members of the general public will be invited to judge the pieces. It's a great opportunity for artists to show off their skills and for more people to take an active interest in local art. The winner in each category will receive £1000.

I'd like you to write an article encouraging people of all ages and abilities to enter the competition.

Thanks very much
Stephanie

Write an article persuading the readers of your magazine to enter the competition.

Remember to:

• Plan your answer.

• Use full sentences and paragraphs. You will be marked on spelling, punctuation and grammar.

You have 25 minutes to complete this exercise. You may use a dictionary.
Write your answer on a separate piece of paper.

(15 marks)

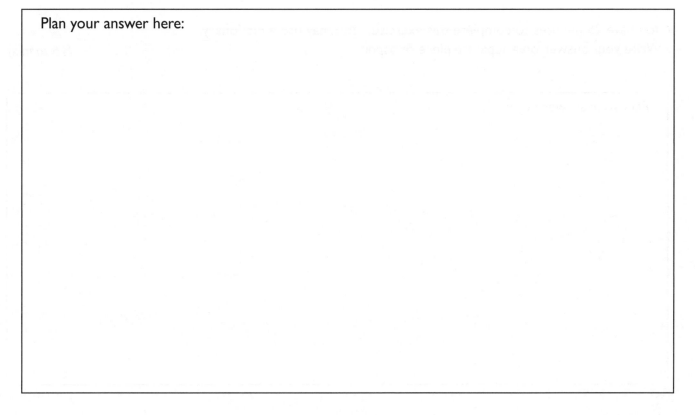

Plan your answer here:

Exercise D — Restaurant Review

You read the advertisement below in your local newspaper, and you and a friend decide to go to the restaurant.

Amalfi

If you want a proper Italian dinner then come to *Amalfi* — the new restaurant on Upper Street. *Amalfi* offers the very best in Mediterranean food at affordable prices. Our specialities include stone-baked pizzas, delicious lasagnes and creamy carbonaras. We've also got live Italian music playing so you'll really get a feel for the Italian culture. Come to *Amalfi* — you'll never taste better Italian food!

Write a review of *Amalfi* for a website about restaurants in your area.

You should include:

• What you enjoyed about your visit.

• Anything you thought that the restaurant could improve.

Remember to:

• Plan your answer.

• Use full sentences and paragraphs. You will be marked on spelling, punctuation and grammar.

You have 25 minutes to complete this exercise. You may use a dictionary.
Write your answer on a separate piece of paper.

(15 marks)

Plan your answer here:

Exercise E — Report on New Airport

You see this article in the local paper.

New Airport Sparks Outrage

Plans to build a new airport near Newtown have divided the local community. Residents are concerned that the new airport will be noisy and cause an increase in pollution. They claim that this will make many people less likely to work, live and shop in Newtown.

However, the Mayor has stated that the airport will lead to better transport links to other towns. She hopes that this will mean that local businesses can sell their products to more people. She also argued that the airport will create more jobs and this will mean more people will live and shop in Newtown.

The shop you work for is based in Newtown. Your manager wants you to write a report about the positive and negative effects that the new airport might have on the shop.

You should include:

- The benefits that the new airport might bring to your shop.

- The disadvantages that the new airport might bring to the shop.

- Whether you think the new airport will help the shop or not.

Remember to:

- Plan your answer.

- Use full sentences and paragraphs. You will be marked on spelling, punctuation and grammar.

You have 25 minutes to complete this exercise. You may use a dictionary.
Write your answer on a separate piece of paper.

(15 marks)

Plan your answer here:

Exercise F — Letter to a Bus Company

This advert for JTL buses is put through your door.

JTL BUSES

We take you where you want to go, and get you there on time.

We promise that:

- Our buses are always on time
- We've got the friendliest drivers around
- Our vehicles are clean and reliable

And best of all... our service is great value for money.
So give us a try today, and ***get on board*** with your local bus service.

JTL buses: 48 Canal Street, Moorewaite, Cumbria, LA10 7FW

You take a JTL bus to work every day and you are unhappy with the service they provide. Write a letter to the company telling them about your complaints.

Remember to:

- Plan your answer.

- Use full sentences and paragraphs. You will be marked on spelling, punctuation and grammar.

- Set your letter out correctly.

You have 25 minutes to complete this exercise. You may use a dictionary.
Write your answer on a separate piece of paper.

(15 marks)

Plan your answer here:

Exercise G — Comment on a Crime Forum

You click on a link for a forum about crime in Britain. You read the two posts below.

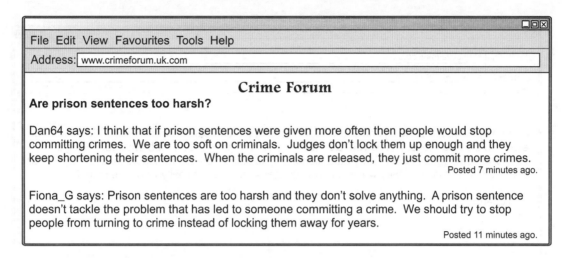

Write your own comment for the Crime Forum giving your detailed views about prison sentences.

Remember to:

• Plan your answer.

• Use full sentences and paragraphs. You will be marked on spelling, punctuation and grammar.

You have 25 minutes to complete this exercise. You may use a dictionary.
Write your answer on a separate piece of paper.   *(15 marks)*

Plan your answer here:

Exercise H — Leaflet for New Employees

You receive the email below at work.

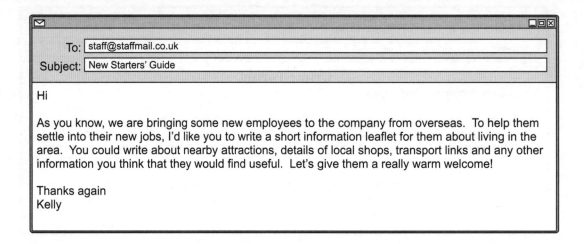

To: staff@staffmail.co.uk

Subject: New Starters' Guide

Hi

As you know, we are bringing some new employees to the company from overseas. To help them settle into their new jobs, I'd like you to write a short information leaflet for them about living in the area. You could write about nearby attractions, details of local shops, transport links and any other information you think that they would find useful. Let's give them a really warm welcome!

Thanks again
Kelly

Write the text for a leaflet informing new starters about the local area.

You should include:

- Activities that they can do in the area.

- Information about public transport.

- Any advice that you think could be helpful.

Remember to:

- Plan your answer.

- Use full sentences and paragraphs. You will be marked on spelling, punctuation and grammar.

You have 25 minutes to complete this exercise. You may use a dictionary.
Write your answer on a separate piece of paper.

(15 marks)

Plan your answer here:

Exercise 1 — Letter of Complaint

You bought some clothes from the company shown below.

Dreams Clothing

Dreams Clothing is a new online clothing store where you can order designer clothes at affordable prices.

We promise:

- Top-quality products
- Unbeatable prices
- The latest fashions
- Speedy delivery

Dreams Clothing — amazingly good-value fashion.

Dreams Clothing, 17 Hart Street, Vicarstown, Southampton, SO1 8BS

You were unhappy with the service you received. Write a letter to the company telling them about your complaints.

You should include:

- What the problem was.
- What you expect the company to do about the problem.

Remember to:

- Plan your answer.
- Use full sentences and paragraphs. You will be marked on spelling, punctuation and grammar.
- Set your letter out correctly.

You have **25 minutes** to complete this exercise. You may use a dictionary.
Write your answer on a separate piece of paper.

(15 marks)

Plan your answer here:

Exercise J — Email to a Friend

You recently visited the hotel below.

The Buttercup Hotel

The Buttercup Hotel, Glinton, is an award-winning hotel in a brilliant location. We offer luxury rooms — without the luxury price tag!

When you stay with us you're only a short walk from a bustling high street with plenty of shops, restaurants and bars. But, if you don't feel like leaving the comfort of the hotel, we've got an on-site restaurant which serves a great range of high-quality dishes from 6.30 am right up to 10.30 pm.

Each room is clean, spacious and comfortable and has free tea and coffee making facilities. Each room is also fitted with a flat screen TV and a DVD player.

Write an email to a friend explaining why The Buttercup Hotel is such a good place to stay.

Remember to:

• Plan your answer.

• Use full sentences and paragraphs. You will be marked on spelling, punctuation and grammar.

• Set your email out correctly.

You have 25 minutes to complete this exercise. You may use a dictionary.
Write your answer on a separate piece of paper.

(15 marks)

Plan your answer here:

Answers to the Writing Questions

Section One — Writing Structure and Planning

Page 69

Q1 a) Audience: tourists
Purpose: to explain what there is to do in your town

b) Audience: your council
Purpose: to complain about the lack of recycling facilities

c) Audience: a charity shop manager
Purpose: to apply for voluntary work

d) Audience: your boss
Purpose: to persuade them to give you flexible working hours

e) Audience: newspaper readers
Purpose: to advise how to save money

Q2 a) Informal
b) Formal
c) Formal
d) Formal
e) Informal

Page 73

Q1 Answers may vary, for example:
Hi everyone
I'd really like to go to a theme park and was wondering who wants to go to Talltown Towers with me?
I was thinking of going on 22nd May. There's a train that leaves at 8 am that would get us to Uxley for 10 am (or if you'd prefer to drive, give me a call and I'll give you directions).
I've heard there are a lot of rides that you'll get wet on, so make sure you bring waterproofs.
If anyone wants to bring other friends, that's fine.
Finally, if we book tickets online, they're half-price.
I think it'll be a really fun day, and I hope you can all come.
Hope to see you soon
Kate

Page 75

Q1 New coffee shops are opening up every day in the UK. It is thought that the number of coffee shops will double in just a few years.

Some people believe that the British interest in coffee began in 1978, when the first coffee shops opened in London. When it became clear that these shops were making a lot of money, more and more began appearing all over the country.

Last year, over two billion pounds worth of coffee was sold. The biggest coffee chains sell just under half a million cups of coffee every day.

However, not everyone likes coffee. Surveys suggest that 16% of the population have never visited a coffee shop.

Section Two — Choosing the Right Language and Format

Page 77

Q1

In your plan you should include:
• Give examples of ways you could help organise the party, for example put up the decorations or book the DJ.
• Any other suggestions you might have for the party. For example, a fancy-dress theme or organising transport home.

In your answer you should:
• Write 'To' and then 'harry. coates@officemail.co.uk'.
• Underneath, write 'From' and then your email address.
• Make sure you fill in the subject box with something suitable, for example 'Help with Christmas Party'.
• Start with a suitable opening, for example 'Hi Harry'.
• Write in paragraphs. You should use the bullet points in the question as a rough guide for what each paragraph should be about. You should use a new paragraph for each bullet point.
• Use an informal writing style because you know him personally.
• End with something like 'Speak to you soon' or 'Thanks' and your name.

Page 79

Q1

In your plan you should include:
• The reasons why you want to volunteer for the Mitterdon Community Centre, for example you want to get some work experience.
• Give examples of experience you have, for example you've done volunteer work in the past.
• Ideas about the sport or craft programme you'd like to run, for example coach a football team or teach mural painting.

In your answer you should:
• Write your name and address at the top right of the page.
• Write the date underneath your address.
• Write the full address of 'Mitterdon Community Centre' on the left-hand side of the page.
• Start with 'Dear Mrs Holt'. Do not use 'Dear Sir / Madam'.
• Use a formal writing style.
• Write in paragraphs. You could have one paragraph about why you want to volunteer for the programme, and another paragraph explaining why you're right for the role. You should use a new paragraph for each bullet point.
• End with 'Yours sincerely', because you know who you're writing to, and your full name.

Page 81

Q1

In your plan you should include:
• What the event was and why it was held, for example a charity dinner hosted by the Jane Bauer Foundation to raise money for the local hospital.
• What happened at the event, for example there was a speech by Mr James Johnson and a raffle.
• That the event was successful, it raised £3,500.

In your answer you should:
• Be formal because you're writing a newspaper article.
• Be informative and mention everything that happened at the event. For example, there were some great raffle prizes, such as a bottle of champagne and a holiday to Venice.

Page 83

Q1

In your plan you should include:
• Some advantages of the new car park. For example, it will mean there are fewer parking problems in Burnham.
• Some disadvantages of the theatre closing. For example, people will have to travel up to 50 miles to see a play.

In your answer you should:
• Be formal because you're writing a report.
• Write an introduction that introduces the issue.
• Include all the advantages and disadvantages of the closure of the theatre and the opening of the car park.
• Organise your information using bullet points or numbered lists, and subheadings.
• Include a conclusion which gives your opinion on the issue. You could write persuasively if you felt strongly one way or the other.

Page 85

Q1

In your plan you should include:
• Information about the office, for example it's friendly and welcoming.
• Information about the area, for example it's in a town where there is plenty to do.
• Some benefits of working for the company, for example you get health insurance.

In your answer you should:
• Be formal because you're writing a leaflet to get people to apply for a job.
• Include plenty of details about the company and the area where the company is located because a leaflet needs to be informative.
• Be persuasive because you're encouraging people to apply for a job at your company.
• Organise your information using bullet points or numbered lists, and subheadings.
• Write in paragraphs. You should use the information in the email and the bullet points in the question as a rough guide for what each paragraph should be about. You should use a new paragraph for each bullet point.

Page 87

Q1

In your plan you should include:
• The reasons why you should be chosen for the holiday, for example you work really hard in your job, but you can't afford a nice holiday.
• You could include worthwhile things you might have done, for example volunteered to work at a youth centre.

In your answer you should:
• Write your name and address at the top right of the page.
• Write the date underneath your address.
• Write the full address you're given on the left-hand side of the page.
• Start with 'Dear Sir / Madam' because you don't know the name of the person you're writing to.
• Use a formal writing style.
• Write in paragraphs. You could have one paragraph about the hard work that you do, and another paragraph explaining why you need a holiday.
• End the letter with 'Yours faithfully', because you don't know the person's name, and your name.

Page 89

Q1

In your plan you should include:
• Your own opinions about recycling, for example you always recycle all your waste.
• The reasons why you feel that way, for example because you are concerned about the environment.

In your comment:
• Make sure you write about the topic in the forum.
• Don't repeat what has been written already, but you can say if you agree or disagree with the comments made by Katie and Ali.
• Give your own opinions on recycling, for example you think that people should recycle, but you don't think they should be imprisoned if they don't.
• Write persuasively because you want to convince readers that your argument is right.
• You can write informally, because it's a forum comment. However, you should write in full sentences and be polite.

Section Three — Using Grammar

Page 91

Q1 a) <u>arrived</u>
b) <u>go</u>
c) <u>wanted</u>
d) <u>likes</u>
e) <u>came</u>
f) <u>work</u>

Q2 a) <u>Rabbits</u>
b) <u>I</u>
c) <u>He</u>
d) <u>The supermarket</u>
e) <u>Anita</u>
f) <u>We</u>

Q3 a) <u>early</u>
b) <u>every day</u>
c) <u>at 6 pm</u>
d) <u>on Tuesdays</u>
e) <u>in the mornings</u>
f) <u>next week</u>

Q4 a) <u>an Italian restaurant</u>
b) <u>Norway</u>
c) <u>the Arctic</u>
d) <u>the art gallery</u>
e) <u>the living room</u>
f) <u>the shop</u>

Q5 Answers may vary, for example:
Yesterday my cat went missing. She is small, long-haired and black and white. She was last seen in the garden. If you have any information, please let me know.

Page 93

Q1 a) or
b) because
c) so
d) but
e) or
f) and
g) because
h) so

Q2 Answers may vary, for example:
Hi Jamie
Thank you for the invite to dinner and the concert. I'll come for dinner <u>but</u> I can't stay for the concert <u>because</u> I have to pick my brother up from work, <u>so</u> I'll need to leave at about 10 pm.
See you later
Ben

Page 95
Q1 a) therefore
b) however
c) for example
d) therefore
e) for example
f) however

Q2 a) Firstly
b) for example
c) Secondly
d) However
e) Therefore

Page 99
Q1 a) Sarah <u>walked</u> to the park.
b) She <u>had</u> pasta for dinner.
c) I <u>saw</u> a field of sheep on the way to work.
d) He <u>asked</u> her for a lift to the station.
e) We <u>went</u> to the festival.

Q2 a) writes
b) wears
c) have
d) was
e) go
f) play
g) does
h) bake

Q3 a) I <u>will make</u> an apple crumble.
b) He <u>will come</u> to football practice.
c) They <u>will be</u> angry.
d) The horse <u>will eat</u> lots of grass.

Page 101
Q1 a) There <u>is</u> one cat.
b) James <u>doesn't</u> work on Mondays.
c) We <u>were</u> on the train to London.
d) The men <u>have been</u> on holiday.

Q2 a) She <u>might have</u> broken her leg.
b) They <u>could have</u> cleaned the house.
c) I <u>should have</u> gone with him to the bank.

Section Four — Using Correct Punctuation

Page 103
Q1 a) <u>T</u>he trees in <u>S</u>cotland were about 50 ft high<u>.</u>
b) <u>O</u>n <u>M</u>onday he slipped and fell over crossing the river<u>.</u>
c) <u>H</u>iking isn't much fun with the wrong shoes<u>.</u>
d) <u>I</u> don't know where he is<u>.</u> <u>H</u>e might have gone shopping in <u>M</u>anchester<u>.</u>
e) <u>P</u>olar bears are known to be violent<u>.</u> <u>I</u> hope we don't see one<u>.</u>
f) <u>H</u>e advertised his sofa in the newspaper<u>.</u> <u>H</u>e sold it for £100<u>.</u>

Q2 a) Why are there so many horror films out at the moment<u>?</u>
b) It turned out that his own brother was the villain<u>!</u> That surprised everyone<u>.</u>
c) We went to see the football last night<u>.</u> The second half was amazing!
d) That's awful<u>!</u> We should do something about it<u>.</u>
e) How can you like that band<u>?</u> I don't think they're any good<u>.</u>
f) They've sold more records this year than last year<u>.</u> How have they done that<u>?</u>
g) There were slugs on the garden path<u>.</u> One crawled in my shoe<u>!</u>

Page 105
Q1 a) You need to add cinnamon<u>,</u> nutmeg and vanilla to the cake mix.
b) The cat<u>,</u> which looked like a stray<u>,</u> was very friendly.
c) James injured his shoulder<u>,</u> so he couldn't go bowling.
d) The bookshop sells biographies<u>,</u> thrillers and romances.
e) Although the cinema was full<u>,</u> it was completely silent.
f) Would you like chocolate chip<u>,</u> vanilla or strawberry ice cream?
g) They were going to go to the concert<u>,</u> but they missed the bus.
h) Alex Johns<u>,</u> who was my best man<u>,</u> never made it to the wedding.
i) Our team reached the finals<u>,</u> so we went out to celebrate.
j) I want chopped onions<u>,</u> lettuce<u>,</u> peppers and tomatoes in my sandwich.
k) Jim and Maher were going to London<u>,</u> but they changed their minds.
l) The flat-pack table<u>,</u> which had instructions with it<u>,</u> was easy to build.
m) The café<u>,</u> which sold lots of different types of tea<u>,</u> was very popular.

Page 107
Q1 a) haven't
b) you'll
c) I'd
d) couldn't
e) you're
f) didn't

Q2 a) The office's car park
b) The child's sweets
c) The burglar's fingerprints
d) The nurse's uniform

Q3 a) <u>It's</u> not surprising that <u>it's</u> fallen over.
b) The team won <u>its</u> final match. <u>It's</u> unbelievable!
c) <u>It's</u> so nice to see your cat and <u>its</u> kittens.

Page 109
Q1 a) Have you read his new book, <u>'Glimpsing Heaven'</u>?
b) It's the first time I've ever seen <u>'The Woman in Blue'</u>.
c) <u>'The Sparkshire Herald'</u> is full of interesting articles.
d) <u>'Come Dance With Me'</u> is my favourite TV programme.

Q2 a) <u>"Happy Birthday!"</u> we all shouted together.
b) <u>"Get out and never come back!"</u> he shouted at us.
c) <u>"Have you got the time?"</u> the old man asked.
d) She said, <u>"I want you to start calling earlier in the evening."</u>
e) <u>"I've forgotten my work boots again,"</u> complained Craig.
f) The supporters shouted, <u>"Come on Hadych! You can do it!"</u>

Section Five — Using Correct Spelling

Page 111
Q1 a) receive
b) science (word is spelt correctly)
c) achieve
d) fierce (word is spelt correctly)
e) friend
f) weird

Q2 Answers may vary, for example:
Because = <u>B</u>ig <u>E</u>lephants
<u>C</u>an <u>A</u>lways <u>U</u>nderstand
<u>S</u>mall <u>E</u>lephants.

Page 113
Q1 a) cinema<u>s</u>
b) Friday<u>s</u>
c) brush<u>es</u>
d) journey<u>s</u>
e) bab<u>ies</u>
f) hal<u>ves</u>
g) reindeer (rein<u>deer</u> doesn't change)
h) monkey<u>s</u>

Q2 a) The boys ate all the peach<u>es</u>.
b) The pupp<u>ies</u> played in the lea<u>ves</u>.
c) Sp<u>ies</u> always carry kni<u>ves</u>.
d) The branch<u>es</u> were burnt to ash<u>es</u>.

Page 115

Q1 a) stopper (word is spelt correctly)
b) hopeful
c) lovely (word is spelt correctly)
d) replay
e) beautiful
f) mislead

Q2 a) He <u>tried</u> to help the <u>jogger</u>.
b) She was <u>famous</u> for her <u>kindness</u>.
c) I am <u>putting</u> this <u>silliness</u> behind me.

Page 117

Q1 a) He will <u>decide</u> where to go <u>tomorrow</u>.
b) <u>Which</u> hotel have you stayed at <u>before</u>?
c) The <u>whole</u> thing was <u>different</u> this time.
d) Do you know <u>when</u> you <u>should</u> call back?
e) <u>Maybe</u> it's just not <u>possible</u>.
f) What is the <u>address</u> of that shipping <u>company</u>?
g) My <u>experience</u> has been <u>horrible</u>.
h) You should <u>know</u> how to act <u>professionally</u>.
i) <u>Thank you</u> for dealing with my <u>complaint</u>.
j) I will <u>definitely</u> use your <u>business</u> again.
k) It <u>may be</u> a leak, but I <u>doubt</u> it.
l) Is it <u>necessary</u> to do this <u>immediately</u>?

Page 121

Q1 a) <u>There</u> is no way to get <u>off</u> this bus early.
b) <u>Are</u> there <u>too</u> many people on board?
c) I hope <u>you're</u> joking when you say <u>you're</u> going to buy a snake.
d) <u>They're</u> going to go <u>to</u> bed.
e) He was <u>being</u> careless with <u>your</u> car.
f) Can you <u>teach</u> me how to use <u>our</u> dishwasher?

Q2 a) They <u>brought</u> <u>their</u> dog into work.
b) <u>They're</u> going <u>too</u> far this time.
c) She wants to <u>teach</u> her son how <u>to</u> be polite.
d) I think <u>you're</u> tired <u>of</u> long hours.
e) I want <u>to</u> <u>learn</u> cooking from an expert.
f) Toby's <u>been</u> to the gym. Have you been going <u>there</u> too?
g) I <u>bought</u> it from that new shop over <u>there</u>.
h) Are <u>your</u> children <u>being</u> naughty?

i) <u>There</u> is the cake I <u>brought</u> into work.

Writing Test Practice

These writing exercises are all worth 15 marks. They each take 25 minutes to complete. Don't forget, different exam boards mark their tests differently. Ask your teacher which exam board you are sitting so you know what to expect in the real test.

Exercise A (Page 123)

You should set your letter out correctly:
• Write your name and address at the top right-hand side of the page.
• Write the date underneath your address.
• Write the full address of 'Car Mechanics Club' on the left-hand side of the page:
Car Mechanics Club
27 Elvet Road
Swindon
Wiltshire
SN1 3LD
• Start with 'Dear Sir / Madam' because you don't know who you're writing to.
• End the letter with 'Yours faithfully' because you don't know the person's name.
(You get 1 mark for using the correct format.)

Your writing style should:
• Be formal because you don't know the person you're writing to.
• Be informative because you want Car Mechanics Club to understand clearly what impressed you.
(You get 1 mark for using a suitable tone and style for your audience.)

You should include this information:
• An explanation of your break down. For example, your car started making a strange noise, so you pulled over to check the engine was all right. At this point smoke started coming out of the front of the car.
• What you like about the service provided by the Car Mechanics Club. For example, you called Car Mechanics Club and they arrived within 20 minutes. The mechanic that helped fix your car was very friendly and explained everything he was doing to the car. He managed to fix the car on the roadside, and you were able to drive away with it an hour later. As a result, you think that the membership price is very good value, and you would recommend the Car Mechanics Club to your friends

and family.
(You can get up to 3 marks for including suitable content.)

You should organise your ideas logically:
• Start with the purpose of the letter, that you're writing to thank them for providing a great service.
• Go on to say what happened to your car when it broke down, and how the Car Mechanics Club helped you.
• End by saying what you're going to do now, for example recommend them to your friends.
(You can get up to 3 marks for ordering your ideas sensibly.)

Use a clear structure:
• Start a new paragraph every time you introduce a new point.
• Write in full sentences.
• Include a range of different sentence structures.
• Write 200-300 words.
(You get 1 mark for using the correct structure.)

You should use correct spelling, punctuation and grammar.
(You can get up to 6 marks for using correct spelling, punctuation and grammar.)

You should be aiming to get around ten marks and above to pass.

Exercise B (Page 124)

You should set your email out correctly:
• Write 'To' followed by louise. fitzgerald@sportmail.co.uk to show who the email is for.
• Underneath, write 'From' and then your email address.
• Write 'Subject' followed by a suitable subject, for example 'Healthy Hearts Trust' or 'Charity Event'.
• Start your email with 'Dear Ms Fitzgerald'.
• Sign off your email with something suitable, for example 'Yours sincerely' and your name.
(You get 1 mark for using the correct format.)

Your writing style should:
• Be formal because you don't know personally the person you're writing to.
• Be persuasive because you want her to help you with your event.
• Be friendly because you want to make a good impression.

Answers to the Writing Questions

(You get 1 mark for using a suitable tone and style for your audience.)

You should include this information:
• What Healthy Hearts Trust does. For example, Healthy Hearts Trust is a charity that helps people fight heart disease. They organise charity events to help raise money to buy hospital equipment and they provide advice to people about keeping their hearts healthy.
• What event you are organising. For example, you are organising a sponsored fun run on 16th July and all money raised will go towards helping buy new heart-scanning equipment for a local hospital.
• How Louise Fitzgerald can promote the charity's work. For example, you think she is one of the country's best runners. Lots of people would take part and raise money if she provided training plans for them and was there to present prizes at the end of the challenge.

(You can get up to 3 marks for including suitable content.)

You should organise your ideas logically:
• Start by explaining what Healthy Heart Trust does.
• Go on to explain in detail the event that you are organising.
• End by saying why you have chosen Louise Fitzgerald to help promote it and how she can help you.

(You can get up to 3 marks for ordering your ideas sensibly.)

Use a clear structure:
• Start a new paragraph every time you introduce a new point.
• Write in full sentences.
• Include a range of different sentence structures.
• Write 200-300 words.

(You get 1 mark for using the correct structure.)

You should use correct spelling, punctuation and grammar.
(You can get up to 6 marks for using correct spelling, punctuation and grammar.)

You should be aiming to get around ten marks and above to pass.

Exercise C (Page 125)

You should set out your article suitably:
• Write a headline to show what the article is about, for example 'Art Competition' or 'Opportunity for Budding Artists'.
• You could use subheadings to break up the text.

(You get 1 mark for using a suitable format.)

You writing style should:
• Be formal because it is for a magazine and you don't know the audience you are writing for personally.
• Be persuasive because you want people to enter.
• Be clear because you want everyone to understand what the competition is about.

(You get 1 mark for using a suitable tone and style for your audience.)

You should include this information:
• When and where the competition will be taking place. For example, the art competition will take place on 4th February in the town hall.
• The purpose of the competition. For example, the art competition's aim is to bring attention to local art and to give budding artists a chance to show off their work. It is open to artists of all ages and abilities.
• Reasons why local artists might want to enter the competition. For example, artists can display their work in the town hall so that the local community can come and see it. There's also a chance that they could win £1000.

(You can get up to 3 marks for including suitable content.)

You should organise your ideas logically:
• Start by describing what the event is, and when and where it will take place.
• Go on to describe the purpose of the competition.
• End by persuading local artists to enter the competition.

(You can get up to 3 marks for ordering your ideas sensibly.)

Use a clear structure:
• Start a new paragraph every time you introduce a new point.
• Write in full sentences.
• Include a range of different sentence structures.
• Write 200-300 words.

(You get 1 mark for using the correct structure.)

You should use correct spelling, punctuation and grammar.
(You can get up to 6 marks for using correct spelling, punctuation and grammar.)

You should be aiming to get around ten marks and above to pass.

Exercise D (Page 126)

You should set out your review suitably:
• Write a headline to show what the review is about, for example 'Fantastic Food' or 'Horrible Music'.
• End with your name to show who wrote the review. You could also include where you are from.

(You get 1 mark for using a suitable format.)

Your writing style should:
• Be descriptive because you want to tell the reader what the restaurant was like in detail.
• You could be persuasive if you felt strongly one way or the other.
• Be the same for all of your review. For example, if you start writing in an informal style, don't write some parts in a formal style.

(You get 1 mark for using a suitable tone and style for your audience.)

You should include this information:
• What you enjoyed about your visit. For example, you had a delicious stone-baked pizza that was very affordable and that the staff were friendly. You could say that the entertainment in the restaurant created a good atmosphere.
• Anything you thought that the restaurant could improve. You could talk about the parts of the meal that you didn't enjoy, for example, your friend ordered a carbonara that was too rich. You could mention that it took a long time to for your meal to arrive.

(You can get up to 3 marks for including suitable content.)

You should organise your ideas logically:
• Start by saying what you liked or didn't like about the restaurant.
• Go on to talk about what the restaurant could improve on.
• End by giving your overall opinion of the restaurant.

(You can get up to 3 marks for ordering your ideas sensibly.)

Answers to the Writing Questions

Use a clear structure:
- Start a new paragraph every time you introduce a new point.
- Write in full sentences.
- Include a range of different sentence structures.
- Write 200-300 words.

(You get 1 mark for using the correct structure.)

You should use correct spelling, punctuation and grammar.

(You can get up to 6 marks for using correct spelling, punctuation and grammar.)

You should be aiming to get ten marks and above to pass.

Exercise E (Page 127)

You should set your report out suitably:
- Write a headline to show what the report is about, for example 'Advantages and Disadvantages of New Newtown Airport'.
- You could use subheadings to separate the two sides of the argument.
- Group similar points together. You could use bullet points or a numbered list to show information more clearly.

(You get 1 mark for using a suitable format.)

Your writing style should:
- Be formal because it is a report for your manager.
- Be informative — make sure you include all of the facts.
- Be clear because you want your manager to understand the advantages and disadvantages clearly.

(You get 1 mark for using a suitable tone and style for your audience.)

You should include this information:
- The benefits that the new airport might bring to the shop. For example, the new airport will provide better links to other towns. This means that the shop would be able to sell its products to more people in other towns.
- The disadvantages that new airport might bring to your shop. For example, a new airport would create more noise and pollution which could affect the shop. It could mean that people might be less likely to work and shop in Newtown so there could be fewer customers.
- Whether you think the new airport will help your shop or not. For example, it might be a benefit because you could expand the shop by selling your products to people who live outside of Newtown. Or, you might think that it would be a disadvantage because the noise and pollution would drive shoppers away.

(You can get up to 3 marks for including suitable content.)

You should organise your ideas logically:
- Start by explaining what the report is about. It is to discuss the effects the new airport will have on the shop.
- Explain all the benefits of the new airport. Then explain all the disadvantages of the new airport.
- End by saying what you think your manager should do and why. For example, whether he should back the campaign for the new airport or start a petition against it.

(You can get up to 3 marks for ordering your ideas sensibly.)

Use a clear structure:
- Start a new paragraph every time you introduce a new point.
- Write in full sentences where suitable.
- Include a range of different sentence structures.
- Write 200-300 words.

(You get 1 mark for using the correct structure.)

You should use correct spelling, punctuation and grammar.
(You can get up to 6 marks for using correct spelling, punctuation and grammar.)

You should be aiming to get around ten marks and above to pass.

Exercise F (Page 128)

You should set out your letter correctly:
- Write your name and address at the top right-hand side of the page.
- Write the date underneath your address.
- Write the full address of JTL Buses on the left-hand side of the page:
JTL Buses
48 Canal Street
Moorewaite
Cumbria
LA10 7FW

- Start with 'Dear Sir / Madam' because you don't know who you're writing to.
- End the letter with 'Yours faithfully' because you don't know the person's name.

(You get 1 mark for using the correct format.)

Your writing style should:
- Be formal because you don't know the person you're writing to.
- Be persuasive because you want the company to fix the problems with the service.

(You get 1 mark for using a suitable tone and style for your audience.)

You should include this information:
- Why you are unhappy with the bus service. For example, you take the bus every morning and it is hardly ever on time. This is frustrating because it means you are often late to work. Also the buses are often dirty which makes the journey unpleasant.
- What you think JTL buses should do about it. For example, give you a free 1-month bus pass and take more care about cleaning their buses.

(You can get up to 3 marks for including suitable content.)

You should organise your ideas logically:
- Start with the purpose of the letter, that you're complaining about the bus service.
- Go on to say what the problem is, and why you're unhappy.
- End with what you want the bus company to do to improve the situation.

(You can get up to 3 marks for ordering your ideas sensibly.)

Use a clear structure:
- Start a new paragraph every time you introduce a new point.
- Write in full sentences.
- Include a range of different sentence structures.
- Write 200-300 words.

(You get 1 mark for using the correct structure.)

You should use correct spelling, punctuation and grammar.
(You can get up to 6 marks for using correct spelling, punctuation and grammar.)

You should be aiming to get around ten marks and above to pass.

Exercise G (Page 129)

You should set your forum comment out suitably:
- Write a heading to show what the forum is about, for example 'Prison Sentences'.
- Write in full sentences.
- Group similar points together.

(You get 1 mark for using a suitable format.)

Your writing style should:
- Be persuasive because you want to convince other readers of your argument.
- Be polite and don't use threatening or aggressive language.

(You get 1 mark for using a suitable tone and style for your audience.)

You should include this information:
- Whether you agree with Dan64's comment. For example, you completely agree with Dan64 because you also think that we are too soft on criminals. Or you disagree with Dan64 because not all criminals commit more crimes once they are released.
- Whether you agree with Fiona_G's comment. For example, you agree with Fiona_G because she says that we need to prevent people from turning to crime instead of putting them in prison. Or you completely disagree with Fiona_G because you think that prisons are a good form of punishment and keep criminals out of our communities.
- Your own opinions about prison sentences. For example, that criminals should be punished, but that we should find other ways to help offenders turn their lives around.

(You can get up to 3 marks for including suitable content.)

You should organise your ideas logically:
- Start by saying whether you agree or disagree with the previous comments.
- Go on to give the details about your own opinions.
- End by explaining what you think could be done to improve the situation.

(You can get up to 3 marks for ordering your ideas sensibly.)

Use a clear structure:
- Start a new paragraph every time you introduce a new point.
- Write in full sentences.
- Include a range of different sentence structures.
- Write 200-300 words.

(You get 1 mark for using the correct structure.)

You should use correct spelling, punctuation and grammar.

(You can get up to 6 marks for using correct spelling, punctuation and grammar.)

You should be aiming to get around ten marks and above to pass.

Exercise H (Page 130)

You should set out your leaflet suitably:
- Use a headline to show what each section of the leaflet is about, for example 'Things to do'.
- You could split the leaflet into sections using subheadings.
- You could use bullet points or numbered lists to break up the text.

(You get 1 mark for using a suitable format.)

Your writing style should:
- Be informative, use clear language and make sure you include all the facts.
- Be friendly because you want to be welcoming and give a good impression.
- Be the same for the whole leaflet. For example, if you start writing in an informal style, don't write some parts in a formal style.

(You get 1 mark for using a suitable tone and style for your audience.)

You should include this information:
- Activities that they can do in the area. For example, you could talk about nearby attractions like museums or theme parks, where to go shopping, interesting walks.
- Information about public transport. For example, you could tell them where the train station is, where you can take a bus to, which websites to visit for more information about prices and timetables.
- Any advice that you think could be helpful. For example, where the best-value restaurants are, how to find good accommodation.

(You can get up to 3 marks for including suitable content.)

You should organise your ideas logically:
- You should group similar information together and put the most important points first.
- Start by explaining what the leaflet is about. It gives information about the local area.
- Go on to give details about what there is to do and how they can travel around the area.
- End with any other helpful advice that you think would benefit the new employees.

(You can get up to 3 marks for ordering your ideas sensibly.)

Use a clear structure:
- Start a new paragraph every time you introduce a new point.
- Write in full sentences where suitable.
- Include a range of different sentence structures.
- Write 200-300 words.

(You get 1 mark for using the correct structure.)

You should use correct spelling, punctuation and grammar.

(You can get up to 6 marks for using correct spelling, punctuation and grammar.)

You should be aiming to get around ten marks and above to pass.

Exercise I (Page 131)

You should set out your letter correctly:
- Write your name and address at the top right-hand side of the page.
- Write the date underneath your address.
- Write the full address of Dreams Clothing on the left-hand side of the page:
Dreams Clothing
17 Hart Street
Vicarstown
Southampton
SO1 8BS
- Start with 'Dear Sir / Madam' because you don't know who you're writing to.
- End the letter with 'Yours faithfully' because you don't know the person's name.

(You get 1 mark for using the correct format.)

Your writing style should:
- Be formal because you don't know the person you're writing to.
- Be informative and tell the reader clearly about your complaint.
- Be polite and reasonable, and don't use threatening or aggressive language.

(You get 1 mark for using a suitable tone and style for your audience.)

You should include this information:
- What the problem was. For example, you were unhappy with Dreams Clothing's service because you bought a T-shirt online last week, and when it arrived, you saw that there was a big hole under one of the arms.
- What you expect the company to do about the problem. For example, you think that it is unacceptable to sell a T-shirt in this condition, and you either want a full refund or a replacement T-shirt.

(You can get up to 3 marks for including suitable content.)

You should organise your ideas logically:
- Start with the purpose of the letter, for example, that you're complaining about a purchase you made last week.
- Go on to say what the problem is and why you're not happy.
- End with what you want Dreams Clothing to do. For example, give you a refund or a replacement.

(You can get up to 3 marks for ordering your ideas sensibly.)

Use a clear structure:
- Start a new paragraph every time you introduce a new point.
- Write in full sentences.
- Include a range of different sentence structures.
- Write 200-300 words.

(You get 1 mark for using the correct structure.)

You should use correct spelling, punctuation and grammar.
(You can get up to 6 marks for using correct spelling, punctuation and grammar.)

You should be aiming to get around ten marks and above to pass.

Exercise J (Page 132)

You should set your email out correctly:
- Write 'To' followed by an email address to show who the email is for.
- Underneath, write 'From' and then your email address.
- Write 'Subject' followed by a suitable subject, for example 'The Buttercup Hotel'.
- Start your email with something suitable, for example 'Hi'.
- Sign off your email with something suitable, for example 'Thanks' and your name.

(You get 1 mark for using the correct format.)

Your writing style should:
- Be informal because you know the person you're writing to personally.
- Be persuasive because you want your friend to go and stay at the hotel.
- Be friendly but don't use any slang or text speak.

(You get 1 mark for using a suitable tone and style for your audience.)

You should include this information:
- Details about the hotel. For example, it's a luxury hotel in Glinton, but it's really good value.
- What you enjoyed about your visit. For example, the hotel was right in the middle of Glinton so the shops were really close by and you were able to go for a drink in the evening and walk back to the hotel.
- Why you think your friend should stay there. For example, you think your friend would really like the food in the hotel's restaurant.

(You can get up to 3 marks for including suitable content.)

You should organise your ideas logically:
- Start by telling your friend some details about the hotel.
- Go on to explain why you really enjoyed your visit.
- End by saying why you think your friend should visit the hotel.

(You can get up to 3 marks for ordering your ideas sensibly.)

Use a clear structure:
- Start a new paragraph every time you introduce a new point.
- Write in full sentences.
- Include a range of different sentence structures.
- Write 200-300 words.

(You get 1 mark for using the correct structure.)

You should use correct spelling, punctuation and grammar.
(You can get up to 6 marks for using correct spelling, punctuation and grammar.)

You should be aiming to get around ten marks and above to pass.

Glossary

Advert

A text type that persuades the reader to do something, for example buy a product.

Alliteration

When words that are close together begin with the same sound.

Apostrophe

A punctuation mark that shows that letters in a word are missing, or that something belongs to someone.

Article

A text type usually found in newspapers or magazines.

Audience

The person or people who read a text.

Bias

When a text isn't balanced and only gives one point of view.

Bullet points

A way of breaking up information into separate points in a list.

Caption

Text that tells you more about a graphic.

Controlled Assessment

A part of the qualification that is taken in class and marked by the teacher.

Descriptive writing

Writing that tells the reader what something is like.

Direct address to the reader

When a writer sounds as if they are talking directly to the reader.

Email

An electronic message sent from one computer to another.

Font

How letters look when they are typed, for example **bold** or *italics*.

Formal writing

A type of writing that sounds serious and professional.

Forum

A web page where people can discuss their opinions on a particular subject.

Graphic

A picture, diagram or chart.

Idioms

Commonly used sayings which have a different set meaning to the literal meaning of the words.

Impersonal writing

Writing that doesn't tell you anything about the writer's personality or opinions.

Informal writing

Writing that sounds chatty and friendly.

Informative writing

Writing that tells the reader about something.

Instructive writing

Writing that tells the reader how to do something.

Irony

When a writer says the opposite to what they mean.

Layout

How a text is presented on the page using different presentational features.

Leaflet

A text type, which is usually given away for free, that gives the reader information about something.

Letter

A text type written to a person, or a group of people, which is sent in the post.

Logo

A graphic associated with a business or product.

Metaphor

A way of describing something by saying it is something else.

Personal writing

Text that is written from a writer's point of view and uses emotional language and opinions. It sounds like it's talking to the reader.

Persuasive writing

Writing that tries to convince the reader to do or feel something.

Prefixes

Letters added to the start of a word which change the word's meaning.

Presentational features

Any part of the text which affects how the text looks, for example colour or bullet points.

Purpose

The reason a text is written, for example to persuade or to inform.

Report

A text type that gives information about something that has happened or might happen.

Rule of three

A list of three words or phrases used to create emphasis.

Silent letters

Letters which you can't hear when a word is said aloud. For example, the 'k' in 'knife'.

Simile

A way of describing something by comparing it to something else.

Slogans

Short, memorable phrases used in advertising.

Statistic

A fact that is based on research or surveys.

Style

The way a text is written, for example formal or informal.

Suffixes

Letters added to the end of a word which change the word's meaning.

Tense

Whether a verb is talking about an action in the past, present or future.

Text type

The kind of text, for example an advert or report.

Tone

The way a text sounds to the reader, for example personal or impersonal.

Verb

A doing or being word.

Web page

A document located on the internet.

Index

A

a lot/alot 116
action words 90
addresses 14, 78
adjectives 4
adverts 14
advising 8
'and' 92
apostrophes 106, 107
are/our 119
arguing 6
articles 15, 71, 80
as well/aswell 116
audience 68, 70

B

'because' 92
'been' 100
been/being 120
bias 12
bold text 18, 30
bought/brought 120
bullet points 8, 16
'but' 92

C

capital letters 102
captions 18
charts 30
checking 72, 122
colours 18
columns 15, 16
commas 104, 105
common mistakes with verbs
        100, 101
commonly confused words
        118-120
comparing texts 34
conclusions 88
controlled assessment 1
could've/could of 100
C-V-C rule 115

D

describing words 4, 86
descriptive writing 4
dictionaries 3
direct address to the reader 20
discussing 6
doing words 96
'done' 100
don't/doesn't 101
double inverted commas 108
double letters 115, 116

E

emails 14, 70, 76
exam board 1
exclamation marks 102

F

facts 4, 6, 10
finding information 26
fonts 18
formal letters 78
formal writing 24, 68
forum responses 71
full sentences 90
full stops 102
Functional Skills 1
future tense 98

G

graphics 18
graphs 30

H

headlines 15, 16
hidden purpose 12
how to use this book 2
'however' 94
humour 12

I

'i' before 'e' rule 110
idioms 22
impersonal writing 24
informal letters 78
informal writing 24, 68
informing 4
instructing 8
inverted commas 108
irony 12
italics 18
it's/its 106

J

joining words 8, 94, 95, 104

K

key words 28

L

layout 30
leaflets 14, 84
letters 14, 70, 78
logo 14

M

magazines 15
main points 28
maybe/may be 116
metaphors 22
multiple-choice questions 36

N

newspapers 15
numbered lists 8, 16, 84

O

of/off 119
opinion 6, 10, 12, 88
'or' 92

P

paragraphs 28, 74, 94
past tense 97, 98
past tense with 'have' 98
P.E.E. 74
personal writing 24
persuading 6, 71, 86
planning 70-72, 74, 90
plurals 112, 113
prefixes 114
present tense 96
presentational features
    16, 18, 30
punctuation 102-109
purpose 4, 6, 8, 12,
    26, 68, 70

Q

question marks 102
quotation marks 108

R

reading test 1
reports 71, 82
reviews 71
rhetorical questions 20
rule of three 20

S

scanning 28, 30
sentences 90
silent letters 116
similes 22
single inverted commas 108
slogans 20
'so' 92
sources 26, 34, 37
speaking and listening 1
spelling tricks 110
statistics 10
style 24, 68
subheadings 15, 16, 80, 84
suffixes 114, 115
summaries 32, 80, 82

T

tables 30
teach/learn 120
tenses 96-98
texts that
    advise 8
    argue 6
    describe 4
    discuss 6
    inform 4
    instruct 8
    persuade 6
text types 14, 15, 76
texts with more than one
    purpose 8
thank you/thankyou 116
their/they're/there 118
'therefore' 94
titles 16, 84
to/too 118
tone 24
tricky spellings 110, 116
twisting statistics 10
types of text 14, 15

U

unbalanced writing 12
understanding information
    28, 30

V

verb agreement 100
verb tenses 96-98
verbs 90, 96-98, 100

W

websites 14
writing articles 80
writing emails 70, 76
writing leaflets 84
writing letters 70, 78
writing reports 82
writing style 68
writing test 1

Y

your/you're 119

E2SRA2